The Venture Compass:

Closing the Gap Between Where You Are and Where You Want To Be

Mark Falzon & Mac Christopherson

The Venture Compass: Navigating the Distance Between Current Reality and Potential / Mark Falzon & Mac Christopherson

ISBN: 978-0-6457675-5-1
eBook ISBN: 978-0-6457675-4-4

For the founders who step into the unknown.
May this Compass help you find your way forward.

AUTHOR'S NOTE

This book began with a simple question:

How do we give founders a map that reveals not only where they are, but where they can go?

The Venture Compass emerged from decades inside ventures, building, scaling, advising, failing, learning and returning with clearer eyes and sharper insight. It grew from patterns we saw again and again across industries, stages and founders, and from a shared belief that clarity should not be a privilege. Founders deserve a way to understand their business structurally, not just emotionally, long before they face the weight of execution.

Thank you for stepping into this work, and for the difference you are making, in your venture, your community and the larger systems your leadership touches. Our hope is that this Compass brings clarity where there is uncertainty, and helps you navigate the distance between your current reality and the potential you can feel but may not yet see.

Mark and Mac

FOREWORD

by Michelle Duval

For more than two decades, I have had the privilege of working closely with thousands of founders, leaders and innovators. I have witnessed the extraordinary courage required to turn an idea into a venture, the psychological complexity of navigating uncertainty, and the immense personal growth demanded of anyone who chooses to build something that did not exist before.

Across all of these experiences, one truth has been consistent:
founders are not short on ambition, creativity or drive; they are short on clarity.

Clarity about what matters most.
Clarity about the real forces shaping their venture.
Clarity about the patterns holding them back.
Clarity about where they are in their own evolution as a leader.

This is why *The Venture Compass* is such an important contribution.

Mark Falzon and Mac Christopherson have distilled decades of lived experience into a framework that is both elegant and deeply practical. They have created a way for founders to see their venture structurally, through nine interconnected forces that influence every decision, every milestone and every outcome.

Their work complements the research and methodology behind Marlee (formerly Fingerprint for Success), where we have spent years mapping the cognitive biases, motivational drivers and behavioural patterns that distinguish successful founders and teams. Where Marlee illuminates the *inner landscape* of human motivation, the Venture Compass illuminates the *outer architecture* of the venture itself.

Together, these two perspectives, the human system and the business system, create a more complete understanding of what is required to build something coherent, scalable and resilient.

What I admire most about this book is its balance.
It is grounded without being heavy.
Simple without being simplistic.
Insightful without losing practicality.
And compassionate without losing strategic rigour.

Mark and Mac have written a book that honours the founder's journey.
They understand the weight founders carry.
They understand the pressure to perform before clarity is earned.
And they understand the emotional and structural patterns that quietly shape every venture's trajectory.

This book gives founders something rare:
a map that is both accurate and humane.

Whether you are just beginning your venture, in the midst of scaling, or navigating a complex period of change, *The Venture Compass* will help you understand your current reality with greater honesty, see your potential reality with greater confidence, and close the Gap between the two with greater precision.

It is a gift to founders and a powerful addition to the body of work supporting entrepreneurship globally.

I am delighted to introduce it.

Michelle Duval
Founder, Marlee (formerly Fingerprint for Success)

ACKNOWLEDGEMENTS

This book would not exist without the founders whose courage, honesty and persistence shaped the development of the Venture Compass™. Every insight in these pages comes from real conversations, real challenges and real victories shared across many years in the arena. Your willingness to be transparent about the complexities of building a venture has been the catalyst for this work.

To the MAD Ambassadors, Board, ecosystem partners and collaborators whose wisdom, pattern recognition and lived experience helped refine the Compass into a tool that serves founders at every stage, thank you for being part of the village behind this movement. Your contribution has strengthened the integrity and clarity of this framework.

To the founders who trusted us with their vision, their challenges and their hopes, this book is written for you. Your commitment to creating something meaningful in the world continually inspires our work.

To the investors, family offices and strategic partners who recognise the value of integrated, structural thinking, your support has helped bring coherence and momentum into a world that deeply needs it.

And finally, to our families, whose encouragement, patience and belief make all this work possible. Thank you for walking alongside us. Your support is the foundation beneath everything we build.

Mark Falzon & Mac Christopherson

COMPASS FOUNDATIONS

The Structural Principles Beneath the Venture Compass

Every venture carries two realities: a current reality and a potential reality. The Compass exists to help founders see the distance between the two with clarity, and to navigate that distance deliberately.

Four structural principles sit beneath the Venture Compass:

1. Internal and External Forces
Every business is shaped by internal dynamics (people, culture, structure) and external forces (markets, timing, competition, regulation). Clarity requires the ability to see both.

2. Hard and Soft Architecture
Hard structure includes capital, pricing, systems, operations and financial mechanics.
Soft structure includes culture, leadership, communication and behaviour.
Alignment between the two creates stability. Misalignment creates friction.

3. Current Reality → Vision → Bridge → Gap
This simple progression, drawn from the Creative Paradigm, underpins the Compass. It helps founders locate themselves in the journey and understand what must shift to reach their potential.

4. Capital Amplifies Whatever Exists
Capital does not fix misalignment. It accelerates it.
Well-aligned businesses gain momentum with capital.
Misaligned businesses hit the wall faster.

These foundations give the Compass its depth, and explain why the quadrants matter, not as theory, but as the structural forces that shape every venture.

TABLE OF CONTENTS

INTRODUCTION

Why Founders Need a Compass

Every visionary founder begins with a sense of possibility. A problem they want to solve. A glimpse of a future reality they can almost see. A feeling that their idea belongs in the world. But building a venture is not a straight line, and the world founders step into, is full of complexity, hidden pressures, mixed signals and an investor landscape that often feels opaque and impenetrable.

Most founders don't struggle because of a lack of courage or creativity. They struggle because they lack a clear way to understand the truth of where their business stands, and a structured way to navigate what comes next. They struggle because fear, urgency, optimism bias and emotional attachment can distort the picture, making the venture look stronger or weaker than it really is, or stretching or shrinking the Gap between today's reality and future potential in ways that are not accurate.

This is where the Venture Compass™ was born.

It began as a response to a gap you can feel across the startup world. Founders put everything into their pitch. They walk into investor meetings with energy, preparation and belief. They walk out with polite encouragement and almost no feedback.

"Thanks for your time. We'll be in touch."
Then silence.

Or a message weeks later:
"You don't quite fit our mandate."
Nothing useful.
Nothing actionable.
Nothing that helps the founder understand what worked, what didn't, or why.

In that gap lies years of unnecessary friction.
And in that gap lies the reason the Venture Compass™ exists.
The Compass gives founders what the investment world rarely offers: **clarity**.

It reveals the eight structural forces that determine whether a business struggles or scales. It shows founders where they are strong, where they are fragile, and what needs to change for the venture to reach its potential. It helps founders prepare long before they raise capital and understand what investors are really seeing when they look at a business.

The Compass does not remove the uncertainty of entrepreneurship. But it removes the guesswork. It replaces the black box with a map.

This book exists for one purpose:
to help founders understand their current reality, identify their potential reality, and see the Gap between the two with practical precision and a clear sense of what it will take to close that Gap.

Because the Gap is not just a conceptual idea, it is the basis of the venture's investment logic. The cost of closing the Gap in time, capability and capital is the investment required to move from where the business is to where it could be. Investors, shareholders and founders all need clarity on this distance, because the expected return on that investment depends on how accurately the Gap is understood.

You will learn:

- what each quadrant measures
- how each quadrant interacts with the others
- why each dimension matters
- how investors interpret what they see
- how founder psychology can distort or clarify the picture
- how to self-assess honestly
- and how to move toward a stronger, more coherent, more investable venture.

This is not a theoretical book.

It is a practical manual drawn from lived work with founders, operators, investors and hundreds of early and growth-stage companies. It is based on the patterns we have seen again and again, the patterns that determine whether a venture finds momentum or stalls.

Throughout this book, you will also see references to simple digital tools that help you go deeper, including a free light-scan of your business and an optional full Venture Compass™ report. These are mentioned lightly, and links throughout the book will take you to the most current versions. The purpose here is to give you clarity, not complexity.

For now, all you need to know is this:

You are holding a map.
A clear way to see where you are,
where you could be,
and how to move from one to the other.

Let's begin.

PART I — ORIENTATION

Chapters 1–3

CHAPTER 1

The Founder's Dilemma

Founders step into the arena with a blend of courage, clarity and hope. They see a problem others overlook. They sense a possibility others dismiss. They carry an idea that feels both weighty and alive. Yet for all this creative intent, most founders quickly discover something confronting and consistent: **the path ahead is far less transparent than the path that led them here.**

There is a moment in every early venture where the distance between vision and reality becomes stark. The idea is strong, the commitment is real, but the clarity is thin. Decisions become harder. The pressure intensifies. Investors and advisors offer encouragement but rarely specificity. The dashboard of the business becomes a swirl of partial signals, contradictory metrics and ambiguous feedback.

This is the founder's dilemma.
Not a lack of intelligence, courage or commitment, but a lack of **clarity**.

Clarity about where the business stands.
Clarity about where the business is heading.
Clarity about what matters now, not later.
Clarity about what investors actually see.
Clarity about which decisions accelerate progress and which quietly stall it.

Founders often feel like they are steering a vessel without instruments. They can sense movement, but not direction. They feel the pressure to grow, but not the guidance to sequence that growth. They know they must present confidently, but rarely receive meaningful feedback on whether their presentation lands.

Most investors don't intend to create this fog. It is simply the nature of their world. They are busy. They see hundreds of decks. They have mandates, biases and internal constraints founders never hear about. They are trained to stay polite, protect optionality and avoid unnecessary conflict. The result is that founders are left without the one thing that could genuinely move them forward… grounded, structured insight.

This lack of clarity doesn't only affect fundraising. It affects every strategic choice inside the business. Without a clear read on the true state of the venture, founders often:

- focus on the visible problem rather than the structural one
- try to "market harder" rather than refine their model
- chase growth before securing foundations
- assume the issue is narrative when the issue is sequencing
- burn precious months on moves that don't shift the trajectory
- misread investor silence as disinterest rather than misalignment

None of this comes from weakness.
It comes from the absence of a map.

Entrepreneurship tests people not because the destination is impossible, but because the territory is uncertain. This is why navigation matters as much as innovation. A founder with a clear understanding of where they are, where they need to go and what the Gap looks like will always move faster and more confidently than a founder relying on instinct alone.

This book begins by acknowledging this dilemma honestly.
You are building something that requires clarity.
You are expected to see your own business with analytical precision.
You are asked to make decisions with consequences measured in years.
And for the most part, you are given very little to work with.

The Venture Compass exists to resolve this.
Not by simplifying the journey, but by revealing it.

The founder's dilemma is not a failing.
It is simply the starting point.

And the Compass gives you the way forward.

CHAPTER 2

The Black Box Problem

Every founder eventually encounters it.

A moment where the work feels invisible, the signals feel thin, and the pathway forward becomes obscured by silence.

You prepare the deck.

You refine your narrative.

You walk into a room with investors, advisors or potential partners.

You bring energy, insight and intent.

And what you receive in return is… almost nothing.

A polite smile.

A nod.

A brief comment about the vision.

A promise to be in touch.

Then, days later, or weeks later, a short message:

"Thank you for your pitch. You don't quite fit our mandate."

No detail.

No context.

No sense of what was missing.

No clarity about whether the issue was the model, the market, the timing, the team, the structure, the narrative or simply internal constraints you could never see.

This is the black box problem.
And it shapes the psychology of early-stage venture far more than most people admit.

Founders are asked to make high-consequence decisions in a system that offers very little meaningful feedback. They are expected to improve, refine and adapt without being told what actually needs improvement, what requires refinement or what is already working. They are asked to pitch into a landscape where the rules are rarely spoken, and the criteria shift subtly from firm to firm, partner to partner, and room to room.

The black box problem creates three quiet forms of distortion:

1. False negatives.
Companies with genuine potential are rejected not because they are weak, but because the investor's mandate, timing or internal process didn't align. Without knowing this, founders assume they failed.

2. False positives.
Companies receive surface-level encouragement, "love what you're doing", but the internal read was far more hesitant. Founders misinterpret politeness as momentum, and lose months pursuing the wrong investors or the wrong strategy.

3. Invisible patterns.

The most important insights, the patterns investors see across hundreds of companies, never reach the founder. The learnings that could shape a stronger business remain sealed inside investment committees and partner discussions founders never witness.

None of this is malicious.

It is the natural outcome of a system where investors must process an overwhelming volume of opportunities while protecting optionality, diplomacy and time.

But for founders, this lack of visibility is costly.

It leads to avoidable mistakes, unnecessary pivots, missed opportunities and prolonged uncertainty. It erodes confidence not because the business is failing, but because the founder cannot see the real picture.

This is the environment in which the Venture Compass was created.

The Compass exists to break open the black box, not by revealing what happens in every investor's meeting, but by revealing the deeper structural forces investors consistently look for, whether they articulate them or not.

It shows founders:

- what matters more than pitch polish
- what investors read between the lines
- what the business fundamentals are actually saying

- where the weak signals are hiding
- where the strong signals can be amplified
- and what needs to shift to turn interest into conviction

The Compass brings light to a process that usually unfolds in shadow.

It gives founders access to the logic behind the decisions, the patterns, the pressures, the risks, the sequencing and the subtle cues investors use to assess readiness.

More importantly, it gives founders a way to improve before the pitch, not after months of silence.

The black box problem is not going away.
But it does not need to remain a barrier.

Clarity dissolves uncertainty.
Structure dissolves distortion.
Insight dissolves unnecessary struggle.

The Compass gives founders what the black box does not:
a way to see clearly, act intelligently and move forward with confidence.

CHAPTER 3

The Origin of the Venture Compass

The Venture Compass did not begin as a theory. It began as a frustration, a very real, very human frustration shared by founders everywhere. Founders were working hard, pitching hard, trying to build something meaningful, yet walking away from investor interactions with almost nothing that genuinely helped them grow.

Across the years, in conversations on the farm, inside companies, in investor rooms and alongside founders at every stage, we kept seeing the same pattern repeating itself.

Founders, the creators and visionaries who see a problem and feel compelled to solve it, would prepare deeply. They would walk into investor meetings with hope and conviction. They would present with clarity, authenticity and intent. They would put their heart on the line.

And after all of that, they would walk away with silence, politeness or feedback so vague it provided no real guidance at all.

It was not merely disappointing.
It was damaging.

Founders would leave those interactions no better informed than when they walked in.

They did not know:

- what landed well,

- what missed the mark,

- what concerned the investor,

- what wasn't aligned,

- or what part of their business needed strengthening.

Most were simply told "not the right mandate" or "not the right time." None of it was actionable.

It was a loop with no learning, a process with no meaningful feedback mechanism, a system that helped no one improve.

We kept seeing this pattern.

And it bothered us because founders deserved better.

We knew the feeling intimately, we had lived it ourselves.

So the question became:

How do we give founders clarity before they step into the investor room?

And beyond that:

How do we give them a way to understand their own business structurally, not just emotionally?

To answer that, we started examining the underlying forces behind the success and failure of ventures we had built, backed or advised. Over time, the same dimensions showed up repeatedly.

Some forces were internal — culture, structure, leadership, people.

Some were external — markets, timing, competition, regulation.

Some were hard — capital strategy, financial architecture, operating systems.

Some were soft — communication, alignment, trust, team dynamics.

All of them were interconnected.

We also saw another repeated truth:

capital amplifies whatever already exists.

If a company is well-structured, capital accelerates growth.

If a company is misaligned, capital accelerates the collision.

A venture can raise capital, but if one quadrant is weak, that money simply helps it hit the wall faster.

So we began codifying the underlying forces shaping a venture's trajectory. And as we worked, one guiding question kept returning:

Where is the business now?

Where could it be?

And what is the Gap between the two?

This simple mapping, current reality, potential reality and the distance between them, became the foundation of the Compass.

From there, the eight quadrants emerged:

- Market Validation
- Market Forces

- Growth Model
- Capital Strategy
- Structure
- Culture
- People
- Integration

And at the centre of it all, the X-Factor, the cohesion, confidence, clarity and narrative alignment that make a company feel investable beyond the numbers.

The Compass was never meant to be theoretical or academic. It was designed to be practical, a tool founders could use to understand themselves, improve their readiness and reduce unnecessary friction on their journey.

It became a way to:
- see the business honestly,
- identify structural weaknesses early,
- amplify what is working,
- sequence the right moves,
- and improve the quality of investor conversations.

From the Compass came the book.
From the book came the reports.
From the reports came the digital tools.

And from those tools came the broader ecosystem of support, including the Mastermind, which sits lightly behind the pages of this work.

But the purpose remains exactly the same as the day this journey began:

To help founders see clearly, decide wisely and move from where they are to where they want to be with greater confidence and coherence.

The Venture Compass gives founders a map.
And now, we step into that map together.

PART II — THE COMPASS

Chapters 4–13

Figure 1 - The Venture Compass™ (Nine-Force Model)

A visual diagram of the eight quadrants surrounding the X-Factor at the centre.

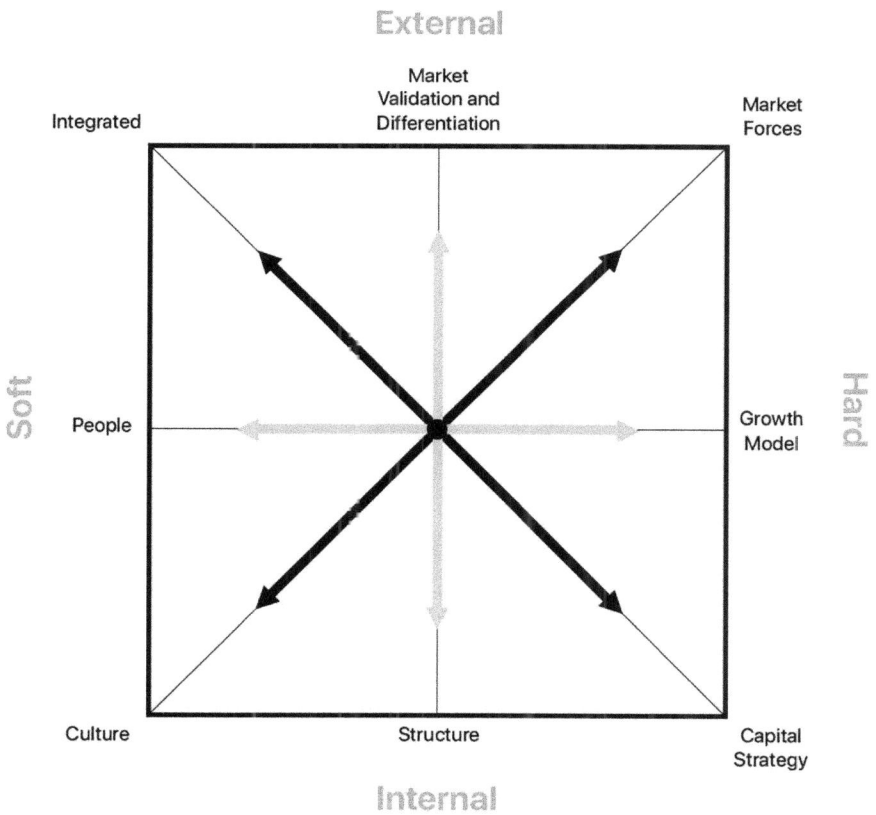

External

Integrated

Market
Validation and
Differentiation

Market
Forces

Soft

People

Growth
Model

Hard

Culture

Structure

Capital
Strategy

Internal

CHAPTER 4

Market Validation & Differentiation

Every venture begins with an idea. But ideas do not build companies, **customers do**. Market Validation is the first and most fundamental force on the Compass because it reveals a truth many founders only discover late in the journey: the strength of the business is not determined by how compelling the idea feels, but by how deeply the market cares.

A founder can be passionate, creative and convinced. They can see the problem clearly and believe in the solution wholeheartedly. But none of that is validation. Validation is not enthusiasm. It is not assumptions. It is not projections or theory.

Market Validation is behaviour.
It is people voting with action, not sentiment.

It answers a single question with radical clarity:

Do people want this, enough to pay for it, use it, and return to it?

This dimension is not simply about whether customers exist. It is about understanding the *quality* of demand, the *intensity* of the problem and the *repeatability* of the behaviour that supports sustainable growth.

Founders often misread this quadrant because psychology shows up early here. Overconfidence, optimism bias and proximity blindness can distort what the market is actually telling them. The Compass brings structure to override that distortion.

CURRENT REALITY

When founders look honestly at this quadrant, they often discover that validation is thinner than they assumed.

Common early patterns include:
- enthusiastic interest but low conversion
- pilot users who do not transition to paying customers
- a small group of loyal customers but no broader signal
- "promising conversations" without revenue
- market size narratives not matched by behaviour
- strong story, weak evidence

These are not failures, they are signals.
They show where the offer resonates and where it has not yet earned commitment.

Key questions to clarify current reality:
- Who is actually buying?
- Why are they buying?
- What behaviour shows this is a priority?
- What friction is slowing conversion?
- What proof exists beyond opinions?

POTENTIAL REALITY

A fully validated venture does not rely on story. It relies on evidence.

Strong potential includes:

- repeatable customer behaviour
- a defined, urgent segment
- consistent conversion
- meaningful retention
- willingness to pay at sustainable margins
- word-of-mouth or product-led referability
- clear early competitive advantage

When validation reaches this level, growth becomes driven by **pull**, not push.

THE GAP

The Gap in this quadrant becomes clear when:

- interest does not match behaviour
- behaviour does not match retention
- retention does not match advocacy
- the story runs ahead of the evidence

In other words, **the narrative is ahead of the behaviour.**

This Gap is structural, not emotional. It shows precisely what must be strengthened before growth, capital or scale will land cleanly.

FOUNDER PATTERNS

Founder psychology frequently shapes how validation is interpreted:

The Optimist

Passionate and belief-driven.

Strength: energy

Risk: hope over evidence

The Analyst

Logical, structured, research-led.

Strength: clarity

Risk: slow to test behaviour

The Practitioner

Close to the problem.

Strength: insight

Risk: projecting personal experience as market reality

Awareness improves accuracy.

INVESTOR LENS

When investors look at Market Validation, they are reading signals that answer five questions:

1. **Is the pain real and urgent?**
2. **Is behaviour repeatable?**
3. **Does the founder understand the market, not just the idea?**
4. **Is there early dominance in a small segment?**
5. **Does validation logically lead to scalable growth?**

Validation is not a checkbox, it is the foundation of credibility.

QUADRANT INTERACTIONS

Market Validation interacts with every other quadrant:

- **Market Forces** — timing shapes behaviour
- **Growth Model** — early revenue must map to mechanics
- **People** — insights depend on how well founders listen
- **Structure** — onboarding and pricing influence conversion
- **Capital Strategy** — strong validation reduces capital intensity

Validation is the first domino.

If it falls well, everything else becomes easier.

MOVES THAT STRENGTHEN THIS QUADRANT

- narrow the segment
- tighten the message
- test pricing early
- reduce friction in activation/onboarding
- measure behaviour, not interest
- listen for complaints more than praise
- anchor messaging in customer language
- focus on depth (one strong segment) before breadth
- validate with real users, not hypothetical enthusiasm

Validation is not a milestone.

It is a pattern.

MICRO EXAMPLES

Weak: "Customers love the idea and said they'd pay for it."

Strong: "We have 37 paying customers, with 22 returning at least three times."

Weak: "People say they'd use it."

Strong: "Our last 10 signups all converted from the same urgent use-case."

MICRO EXERCISE

Validation Reality Check

Write down **three facts (not opinions)** that prove real demand.

If you struggle to find three, the Gap is clearer than you thought.

WHY THIS QUADRANT COMES FIRST

Everything begins here, not with vision, story or product.

A business grounded in behaviour has a foundation.

A business grounded in enthusiasm alone has narrative without structure.

Validation tells the founder what is real.

It tells the investor what is credible.

And it tells the venture where the next step must be taken.

CHAPTER 5

Market Forces

A venture does not grow in isolation. Every company, from the earliest seed idea to the most mature scale-up, sits inside a broader ecosystem of forces that shape its trajectory. Some of these forces are supportive. Some are neutral. Some apply pressure. Some shift suddenly without warning. All of them influence the venture's ability to grow.

Market Forces represent the **external environment** your company operates within. They are the current beneath your feet, the wind behind your back, or the headwind you must push through. They influence every decision you make, every outcome you pursue and every assumption inside your model.

If Market Validation reveals **what customers are doing**, Market Forces reveal **what the world is doing** and how those movements affect the probability of growth.

Founders often misread this quadrant because they want timing to be on their side. Optimism bias, narrative attachment and overconfidence can distort what external signals are actually revealing. The Compass helps override that distortion by grounding interpretation in structure, not hope.

WHY MARKET FORCES MATTER

A great product launched at the wrong moment will stall.

A good business model misaligned with industry shifts will strain.

A strong team inside a contracting market will struggle to gain traction.

Founders often focus their energy internally, product, people, operations, only to discover that external dynamics quietly redefine the opportunity.

This quadrant helps founders see clearly:

- whether the market is expanding or contracting
- whether timing supports or suppresses adoption
- which trends create tailwinds
- which shifts create drag
- what competitors and incumbents influence behaviour
- what invisible forces shape risk and opportunity

Market Forces do not determine destiny,

but they determine the **effort required** to reach it.

CURRENT REALITY

Most founders initially interpret Market Forces based on intuition or narrative momentum. They "sense" the market is big. They "feel" timing is right. They "believe" demand is inevitable.

Instinct is valuable but instinct without evidence is distortion.

The reality becomes clearer when Market Forces are evaluated through observable signals:

Positive or supportive indicators:

- increasing demand in your category
- favourable regulatory shifts
- declining technology or supply costs
- adjacent industries adopting similar solutions
- favourable cultural trends
- increasing partner or ecosystem activity

Negative or resistant indicators:

- a saturated category
- entrenched incumbent strength
- customer budgets tightening
- regulatory barriers increasing
- long procurement cycles
- macroeconomic constraints
- cultural shifts reducing relevance

These signals help calibrate ambition and sequence.

POTENTIAL REALITY

Potential emerges when founders develop a **structured,** not intuitive, understanding of the ecosystem.

Strong potential looks like:

- clarity on category dynamics
- strategic alignment with emerging tailwinds

- understanding where adoption is heading (not just where it is today)
- positioning in the earliest expanding segment
- early advantage in a market about to inflect
- ability to ride a wave rather than create one alone

When Market Forces align with Market Validation, growth becomes **easier, cleaner and more efficient**.

THE GAP

Market Forces Gaps occur when the founder's **story about the market** does not match the **reality of the market**.

Common patterns:
1. **Overestimating TAM**
2. Big market ≠ big opportunity for you.
3. **Misreading timing**
4. Being early feels visionary until cash runs out.
5. **Ignoring structural constraints**
6. Procurement cycles, regulation, switching cost.
7. **Undervaluing incumbents**
8. Incumbents can move faster than expected.
9. **Missing adjacent threats**
10. New entrants reshaping category logic.

The Gap here is often about *alignment*, not effort.

A small move in positioning or timing can collapse a large distance.

FOUNDER PATTERNS

Founders approach Market Forces from three orientations:

1. The Enthusiast

Sees tailwinds everywhere.

Strength: early movement

Risk: narrative over evidence

2. The Skeptic

Sees barriers first.

Strength: risk awareness

Risk: slow to seize windows

3. The Ecosystem Reader

Balances opportunity with evidence.

Strength: strategic timing

Risk: occasional over-analysis

Awareness brings balance.

INVESTOR LENS

Investors read Market Forces quickly and often silently.

They are asking:

- Is this a market turning upward or downward?
- Is timing in or out of phase?
- Is customer adoption accelerating, stable or flat?
- Are there macro shifts that make this inevitable?

- Are there structural headwinds this team can't control?
- Does the founder understand *why now*?

Investors need believable alignment, not certainty, but coherence.

QUADRANT INTERACTIONS
Market Forces influence:

- **Market Validation** — timing amplifies or suppresses behaviour
- **Growth Model** — cost curves and adoption cycles influence economics
- **Capital Strategy** — investor appetite rises and falls with market cycles
- **Structure** — external constraints shape internal readiness
- **Integration** — cultural and regulatory shifts shape expectations

Understanding the environment reduces friction.

MOVES THAT STRENGTHEN THIS QUADRANT

- map structural forces for the next 3–7 years
- watch downstream and adjacent markets
- identify segments adopting earliest
- understand regulatory signals
- evaluate incumbents honestly
- build practical timing assumptions
- test small bets to confirm timing
- differentiate between noise and durable trends

A company aligned to timing moves with less strain.

MICRO EXAMPLES

Weak: "The market is huge."

Strong: "A regulatory shift in 2026 forces every operator to adopt solutions like ours."

Weak: "Competitors are slow."

Strong: "Two incumbents just increased product velocity, this shapes our positioning."

MICRO EXERCISE

Timing Reality Check

Write one line for each:

- **Why now?**
- **Why not three years ago?**
- **Why not three years from now?**

This reveals whether timing is an advantage, a risk or a neutral factor.

Understanding Market Forces is not about prediction.

It is about awareness.

Awareness reduces risk.

And when awareness is structural, the company moves with coherence rather than hope.

CHAPTER 6

Growth Model

A venture can have a strong idea, clear validation and favourable tailwinds, but without a Growth Model that is coherent, scalable and economically sound, the business will strain under its own weight. Growth is not a mystery. It is not luck. It is a set of mechanics, logical, observable and repeatable, that determines how a company expands.

Founders often speak about growth as an aspiration.
Investors view growth as a **system**.

The Growth Model is where those two perspectives converge or collide.

At its core, the Growth Model answers three questions:
1. **How does the business reliably acquire customers?**
2. **How does the business convert and retain them?**
3. **How does the business generate sustainable, expanding econom-ics over time?**

It is the engine of the venture.
If the engine is strong, capital accelerates momentum.
If the engine is weak, capital accelerates instability.

WHY THIS QUADRANT MATTERS

A company can grow in the short term through founder hustle, discounts, grants or personal networks. But sustainable growth, the kind that attracts investment and compounds value, comes from structure.

A strong Growth Model:

- improves conversion
- strengthens retention
- increases margin
- reduces capital intensity
- stabilises culture
- creates predictability
- compounds momentum
- reduces execution risk

A weak Growth Model creates:

- volatility
- reactive decision-making
- high burn
- founder dependency
- unpredictable performance
- operational fatigue

Growth is only as strong as the system beneath it.

CURRENT REALITY

In early stages, growth patterns are usually inconsistent and dependent on founder effort. These signals are real but fragile.

Common early patterns include:

- customer acquisition dependent on the founder
- inconsistent revenue
- low repeat usage
- unclear activation patterns
- high churn
- reliance on pilots rather than paid behaviour
- CAC unstable and unpredictable
- retention disguised by new customer flow
- pricing not aligned to value

These patterns are not red flags.

They are early-stage truths.

The current reality becomes clearer when the founder asks:

- What is the real acquisition pathway?
- What triggers activation?
- Where does churn occur?
- What is our repeat behaviour?
- What is predictable versus effort-based?
- How clean is our pricing logic?

Founder psychology often distorts this quadrant, optimism bias, overconfidence and narrative momentum can make weak growth feel stronger than it is. Evidence dissolves distortion.

POTENTIAL REALITY

A strong Growth Model is repeatable, measurable and scalable.

Potential looks like:

- consistent customer acquisition
- defined activation moments
- strong and improving retention
- expanding margins
- positive unit economics
- customers becoming multipliers
- predictable revenue patterns
- an engine that grows without founder intervention

When this state is reached, growth becomes **design-led**, not effort-led.

THE GAP

The Gap in this quadrant is one of the most consequential.

It often reveals whether growth is:

- engineered
- accidental
- fragile
- or scalable

Common Gap patterns:

1. **Early traction mistaken for scalable traction**
2. **CAC seen as "normal for early stage" rather than a signal**
3. **Retention masked by top-of-funnel wins**

4. **Pricing misaligned with economics**
5. **Founder-led sales interpreted as market-led growth**
6. **Pilots interpreted as demand**

The Growth Gap is not emotional.

It is mechanical.

A founder who understands this Gap can recalibrate growth with precision and speed.

FOUNDER PATTERNS

Founders tend to fall into one of three orientations:

1. The Builder

Product-first, execution strong.

Risk: no scalable acquisition pathway.

2. The Promoter

Great storyteller, strong top-of-funnel.

Risk: weak retention and economics.

3. The Architect

Systems thinker, balanced.

Risk: over-designing early mechanics.

Awareness increases accuracy.

INVESTOR LENS

Investors read growth differently from founders.

They look for:

- repeatability
- quality of revenue
- strong retention
- scalable mechanics
- stable unit economics
- low dependency on founder
- evidence over enthusiasm

Investors don't just ask, "Are you growing?"
They ask, "Can this growth compound without breaking the business?"

QUADRANT INTERACTIONS

Growth Model interacts deeply with:

- **Market Validation** — weak validation makes growth expensive
- **Market Forces** — timing shapes CAC and adoption
- **Capital Strategy** — determines capital intensity
- **Structure** — determines scalability
- **People** — determines execution velocity
- **Culture** — determines quality and consistency

Growth does not happen in isolation.
It happens when the system is aligned.

MOVES THAT STRENGTHEN THIS QUADRANT

- identify and measure activation
- focus on retention before top-of-funnel expansion
- build clear pricing architecture
- understand customer behaviour beyond opinion
- reduce leak points in the funnel
- design repeatability
- validate channels slowly
- build systems that reduce founder dependency

Growth is an engine.

Not a story.

MICRO EXAMPLES

Weak: "We grow through word of mouth."

Strong: "Seventy percent of new customers come through a structured partner channel we can scale nationally."

Weak: "Our churn isn't bad."

Strong: "Our churn is 22%, and closing the onboarding Gap could cut it in half."

MICRO EXERCISE

Growth Clarity Prompt

Complete this sentence:

"We acquire customers through X, convert them through Y and retain them through Z."

If you can't complete it in one breath, the Growth Model isn't clear.

A strong Growth Model is not accidental.

It is built with clarity, grounded in evidence and strengthened through deliberate sequencing.

When the engine is healthy, every other quadrant becomes easier and capital becomes a multiplier rather than a strain.

CHAPTER 7

Capital Strategy

Capital is often misunderstood. Founders tend to see capital as fuel, the resource that enables growth, hiring, product development and expansion. Investors see capital differently. To them, capital is a commitment, a structured decision, and a risk-adjusted bet on the venture's ability to bridge the Gap between its current reality and its potential reality.

Capital amplifies whatever already exists.
If the business is aligned, capital accelerates progress.
If the business is misaligned, capital accelerates instability.

This makes the **Capital Strategy** quadrant one of the most consequential in the Compass. It reveals how capital should enter the business, when it should enter, why it should enter and what structure best supports the company's next stage of growth.

A strong Capital Strategy aligns three things:
1. **the real needs of the business,**
2. **the timing of the business,**
3. **the type and structure of capital.**

When these align, capital amplifies coherence.
When they don't, capital amplifies tension.

WHY THIS QUADRANT MATTERS

Capital is not neutral.

It shapes:

- pace
- priorities
- hiring decisions
- leadership behaviour
- burn rate
- expectations
- pressure
- sequencing

When used well, capital creates:

- stability
- operating capacity
- confidence
- strategic expansion
- capability uplift
- investor trust

When used poorly, capital creates:

- burnout
- noise
- misalignment
- rushed decisions
- strategic drift

Capital is only valuable when it is matched to the true stage of the business and the true shape of the Gap.

CURRENT REALITY

In the early stages, founders often raise reactively rather than strategically. This is where psychology can distort the plan, fear, urgency and optimism bias can create inaccurate reads on what capital is actually needed and why.

Common early-stage patterns include:
- raising for survival rather than strategy
- unclear or overly broad use-of-funds
- capital structure mismatched to model type
- valuations not grounded in fundamentals
- raising from investors misaligned with stage or category
- raising too early without validation
- raising too late after burn rises
- overestimating what capital alone can fix

These patterns are not signs of incompetence, they are signs of inexperience in a high-ambiguity environment.

The current reality becomes clearer by asking:
- What will this capital actually unlock?
- What capabilities must this capital build?
- What milestones will it enable?
- What cannot happen if we raise nothing?

- What risks come with this structure?
- How does this raise connect to our Gap?

Clarity dissolves noise.

POTENTIAL REALITY

A strong capital strategy has coherence, logic and intent.

Potential in this quadrant looks like:
- clear milestone-based capital planning
- a structured use-of-funds aligned to the next stage
- realistic understanding of burn and runway
- investor expectations aligned to stage and model
- capital used to strengthen foundations, not patch symptoms
- the right structure (equity, structured equity, venture debt, revenue-based finance, catalytic capital)
- a capital plan that matches the venture's Gap and sequence

When a venture reaches this state, capital becomes **a strategic accelerator**, not a pressure amplifier.

THE GAP AND CAPITAL

Seed, venture and strategic investors make capital decisions using a simple logic:

Does the expected ROI justify the cost of closing the Gap?

This is why Gap clarity is essential.

Founders often misjudge:

the size of the Gap,

- the cost of bridging it,
- the capability required,
- the time required,
- and the sequence needed.

Optimism bias and urgency distort these reads.

Investors fund **Gap closure**, not optimism.

A founder who can articulate their Gap in grounded, structural terms instantly increases investor confidence.

THE GAP DISTORTION PATTERNS

Overstating the Gap

- inflated potential
- unrealistic timelines
- undervaluing required capability
- underestimating cost to execute
- creates over-raising, over-building and instability

UNDERSTATING THE GAP

- raising too little
- avoiding structural rebuilds
- underestimating effort
- failing to develop leadership capability
- creates chronic underfunding

The Compass stabilises both by grounding the capital conversation in structure, not sentiment.

FOUNDER PATTERNS

Founders approach capital from three instinctive orientations:

1. The Hunter

Always raising, always pitching.

Strength: energy

Risk: misalignment, dilution

2. The Protector

Avoids raising, relies on frugality.

Strength: discipline

Risk: undercapitalisation, missed timing

3. The Designer

Raises intentionally with structural logic.

Strength: coherence

Risk: slower if overly cautious

Awareness improves decision quality.

INVESTOR LENS

When investors evaluate Capital Strategy, they are assessing:

- capital efficiency
- milestone logic
- structure fit
- clarity of use-of-funds

- founder maturity
- risk distribution
- Gap accuracy
- how capital amplifies (or strains) current mechanics

Investors are not asking for perfection, they are asking for **coherent sequencing.**

QUADRANT INTERACTIONS

Capital Strategy interacts deeply with:

Growth Model — determines capital intensity

- **Structure** — determines readiness to absorb capital
- **People** — impacts hiring capacity
- **Culture** — pressure shifts dynamics
- **Validation** — reduces risk
- **Integration** — influences responsible scaling

Capital magnifies whatever is present.

MICRO EXAMPLES

Weak: "We need $1m to keep going."

Strong: "We need $1m to hit $2m ARR, complete three critical hires that halves capital intensity and unlock a debt facility for further runway."

Weak: "We're raising so we can grow faster."

Strong: "We're raising to close the model stability Gap and reduce churn from 27% to under 10%."

MICRO EXERCISE (LIGHT, FOUNDER-FRIENDLY)

Capital Clarity Prompt

Write one sentence answers to these questions:

What is the capital we need and what will we deliver with it?

What is the cost of the capital we are utilising?

If the sentences are unclear, the capital strategy is unclear.

MOVES THAT STRENGTHEN THIS QUADRANT

- raise for strategy, not survival
- align capital type with model type
- define milestone logic before raising
- build capability alongside capital
- raise enough to reach the next structural milestone
- avoid raising during chaos, stabilise first
- align expectations early
- ensure use-of-funds ties directly to Gap closure
- treat capital as a lever, not a lifeline

Capital does not create success.

It amplifies alignment.

Clarity in this quadrant protects the founder, strengthens the business and accelerates the path toward the business's potential reality.

CHAPTER 8

Structure

Every venture has a structure. Whether consciously designed or unconsciously inherited, structure determines how a business performs under pressure, how it scales under demand and how it absorbs complexity. Structure is not the visible product, brand or vision. It is the architecture beneath, the contracts, pricing, margins, systems, governance, decision pathways and operating rhythm that hold everything together.

Founders often underestimate this quadrant because structure is quiet. It rarely screams for attention until the business begins to strain. Yet structure is one of the strongest predictors of whether growth becomes stabilising or destabilising.

Structure answers a simple question:

Can the business hold the weight of the growth it desires?

Founder psychology often distorts this view. Optimism bias, proximity blindness and narrative attachment can make structure feel "fine for now," even when it is already creaking. The Compass clarifies what is invisible until it breaks.

WHY THIS QUADRANT MATTERS
Structure is everywhere in the business:

- pricing
- margins
- legal setup

- governance
- risk
- process
- delivery systems
- operating rhythm
- systems and tools
- financial architecture
- incentives

A strong structure:

- reduces friction
- improves margin
- stabilises performance
- accelerates decision-making
- increases investor confidence
- strengthens culture
- reduces burn
- makes growth cleaner

A weak structure creates:

- rework
- chaos
- burnout
- unclear ownership
- margin erosion
- founder dependency
- operational collapse at scale

Structure is the difference between motion and momentum.

CURRENT REALITY

In early stages, structure is often improvised and that is normal. But improvisation stops working as complexity rises.

Common early structural patterns include:

- pricing that was guessed
- margins unknown or unstable
- processes undocumented
- governance informal
- unclear roles or responsibility drift
- operational bottlenecks
- deliverables dependent on single individuals
- systems that do not scale
- decisions made repeatedly instead of rhythmically

These are not failures.
They are early-stage truths.

Key questions that reveal current reality:

- Are our economics stable or variable?
- Do we know our real contribution margins?
- Does the organisation have clear ownership?
- Where do decisions stall?
- What breaks under increased load?
- What effort is repeating unnecessarily?

Founder psychology often avoids structural work because it feels "slower," but structural improvements often provide the highest ROI.

POTENTIAL REALITY

A strong structural state includes:

- clear, rational pricing aligned to value
- stable and healthy margins
- consistent unit economics
- documented processes
- predictable operating rhythm
- governance that supports decisions
- role clarity
- scalable systems
- low operational risk
- alignment between structure and growth strategy

When structure is strong, everything becomes easier, hiring, leadership, execution, sales, product, culture and growth.

THE GAP

The Structure Gap appears when the **business being built** does not match the **structure required** to support it.

Common Gap patterns:

- pricing mismatch
- margin instability
- weak financial architecture

- fragile delivery systems
- unclear decision rights
- role confusion
- lack of process design
- systems breaking under load
- risk not accounted for

Many of these look small but carry a **high ROI** when corrected. Small structural moves can collapse a large Gap.

FOUNDER PATTERNS

Founders tend to fall into three structural instinct types:

1. The Improviser

Strength: speed

Risk: operational fragility

2. The Architect

Strength: clarity and precision

Risk: over-building too early

3. The Builder

Strength: balanced evolution

Risk: being late to formalise

Structure requires proportional design, not too early, not too late.

INVESTOR LENS

Investors read structure very quickly.

They look for:

- stable margins
- clear economics
- predictable operations
- scalable processes
- strong governance
- low operational risk
- coherence between story and structure

Investors quietly ask:

"Will this company break before it grows?"

A founder who understands their structure builds trust immediately.

QUADRANT INTERACTIONS

Structure interacts deeply with:

- **Growth Model** — weak structure increases CAC and lowers retention
- **Capital Strategy** — structure dictates how capital is used
- **People** — structure shapes performance
- **Culture** — structure sets behavioural expectations
- **Market Validation** — pricing and delivery influence conversion
- **Integration** — structure ensures responsible scale

Structure is the frame that stabilises everything else.

MOVES THAT STRENGTHEN THIS QUADRANT

- redesign pricing
- tighten margins
- document core processes
- simplify decision pathways
- introduce operating rhythms (weekly–monthly–quarterly)
- strengthen governance
- reduce single points of failure
- align incentives with outcomes
- build systems proportional to stage

Structure is not bureaucracy.

It is clarity.

MICRO EXAMPLES

Weak: "The org chart is evolving."

Strong: "Ownership is clear for product, growth and operations and decisions move through a simple weekly rhythm."

Weak: "Margins are improving."

Strong: "Contribution margin is now 42%, up from 27%, after restructuring pricing."

MICRO EXERCISE

Structural Reality Check

Write down the three decisions that took the longest in the last month.

These delays usually reveal the structural Gap.

A well-designed structure reduces friction, increases momentum and strengthens execution.

When structure aligns with strategy, the business begins to move with stability, ease and coherence.

CHAPTER 9

Culture

Every company has a culture. Whether intentionally shaped or unconsciously absorbed, culture determines how people behave when no one is watching, how they respond when pressure increases and how they repair when something breaks. It shapes communication, decision-making, accountability and the emotional tone of the organisation.

Culture is not the poster on the wall.
It is the lived experience inside the company, the tone, rhythm and energy that shape daily behaviour.

Founders often underestimate this quadrant because culture is invisible until it strains. But once the pressure rises, culture becomes one of the most decisive forces in the business.

Culture answers a vital question:
Can this team move together through complexity?

Founder psychology deeply influences culture. Avoidance, overprotection, narrative attachment and emotional blind spots often shape culture long before the founder realises it. The Compass helps reveal these patterns objectively and early.

WHY THIS QUADRANT MATTERS

Culture is not a "soft dimension."

Culture is a **performance dimension**.

A strong culture:

- increases speed
- reduces friction
- supports better decisions
- strengthens retention
- stabilises leadership
- increases trust
- reduces emotional noise
- improves execution
- amplifies alignment

A weak culture:

- slows everything down
- creates confusion
- increases conflict
- drives rework
- undermines trust
- fractures execution under pressure

Culture is the emotional infrastructure of a company.

It determines whether people feel safe enough to be honest and strong enough to perform.

CURRENT REALITY

In the early stages of a venture, culture is often shaped by the founder's presence. This feels natural and energetic, but it also hides deeper patterns.

Common early cultural patterns include:

- founder as emotional centre
- unspoken expectations
- inconsistent communication
- conflict avoidance
- unclear decision rights
- high enthusiasm, low stability
- overreliance on individual heroics
- values declared but not consistently practised

These patterns are normal.
They only become problematic when the venture grows and the founder cannot personally transmit culture through daily contact.

Culture becomes visible when the founder steps back, not before.

POTENTIAL REALITY

A strong cultural state includes:

- psychological safety
- constructive conflict
- consistent communication
- clarity of expectations

- shared language
- healthy accountability
- alignment between incentives and behaviour
- leadership that sets tone and pace
- a team that learns quickly and responds well under pressure

When culture reaches this state, it becomes a competitive advantage.

Teams move faster.

Problems surface earlier.

Repair is cleaner.

Decisions improve.

Trust compounds.

THE GAP

The Culture Gap appears when the **culture the founder believes exists** does not match the **culture the team actually experiences.**

Common patterns:
1. **Declared values not lived in behaviour**
2. **Avoiding hard conversations**
3. **High enthusiasm masking fatigue**
4. **Unclear roles creating hidden tension**
5. **Misaligned incentives**
6. **Fragmented communication**
7. **Founder dependency replacing team capability**

These are not moral issues.

They are structural issues in the emotional system of the company.

Small cultural Gaps often offer very high ROI, one conversation, one expectation set, one rhythm shift can create disproportionate stability.

FOUNDER PATTERNS
Culture often reflects the founder's instinctive pattern:

1. The Driver
Intensity, high pace.
Strength: momentum
Risk: fear-based execution

2. The Supporter
Warm, relational.
Strength: loyalty
Risk: avoidance of accountability

3. The Aligner
Balanced, steady.
Strength: resilience
Risk: stretched under rapid growth

Culture becomes healthy when the founder understands their own influence.

INVESTOR LENS
Investors read culture within minutes.

They watch for:
- coherence in how the team communicates
- clarity in decision-making
- emotional maturity under pressure

- leadership stability
- consistency between values and behaviour
- trust dynamics

Investors know a fractured culture undermines even the strongest model.

A strong culture reassures them the venture can handle scale.

QUADRANT INTERACTIONS

Culture interacts with:

- **People** — capability depends on environment
- **Structure** — structure reinforces cultural norms
- **Growth Model** — culture shapes execution
- **Capital Strategy** — capital pressure changes tone
- **Validation** — cultural openness improves customer insight
- **Integration** — culture influences how responsibly the business scales

Culture is the connective tissue of the Compass.

MOVES THAT STRENGTHEN THIS QUADRANT

- make expectations explicit
- establish consistent communication rhythms
- clarify decision rights
- enable healthy conflict
- balance safety with accountability
- build repair mechanisms

- align incentives with behaviour
- avoid heroics by distributing leadership
- reinforce values through action
- evolve culture as the company grows

Culture is not something you "fix."
It is something you build, deliberately, consistently and with integrity.

MICRO EXAMPLES

Weak: "We have strong values."
Strong: "We run weekly post-mortems, document decisions and track our learning velocity."

Weak: "Our team gets along well."
Strong: "We surface tension early and resolve issues within 48 hours."

MICRO EXERCISE

Culture Reality Prompt

Write down the last **three hard decisions** your team made and the process used to come to a decision.
The pattern tells you what your culture actually is.

A strong culture does not eliminate challenge.
It gives your team the strength to meet challenge with maturity, clarity and coherence.

CHAPTER 10

People

Every venture rises or falls on the strength, alignment and maturity of its people.

Ideas matter.

Models matter.

Capital matters.

But it is people who execute, communicate, adapt, make decisions, solve problems and bring the vision to life.

People are not resources.

They are **vectors**, each with direction, velocity and impact.

A company is not the sum of its headcount.

It is the sum of the vectors inside it, and how well those vectors align.

Founder psychology often distorts this quadrant more than any other. Emotional attachment, proximity blindness, overconfidence, loyalty bias and the tendency to equate team harmony with team capability frequently cloud what is actually happening. The Compass brings structural clarity to the reality of the team, not the story.

People answer the question:

Does this team have the capability and coherence to take the venture where it needs to go?

WHY THIS QUADRANT MATTERS

People determine:

- how decisions are made
- how conflict is handled
- how quickly problems surface
- how effectively they are resolved
- how well information flows
- how the culture holds under pressure
- how execution quality remains consistent
- how customers are treated
- how the business responds to change

Even the best strategy collapses under weak execution. And execution collapses under weak teams.

A strong People quadrant builds:

- trust
- clarity
- capability
- accountability
- stability
- adaptability
- leadership depth

A weak People quadrant creates:

- confusion
- reactivity

- bottlenecks
- emotional volatility
- inconsistent delivery
- decision paralysis

People are the living system of the venture.

CURRENT REALITY

In early stages, team structure is often informal and dependent on founder energy. This feels fast and flexible, but it conceals risk.

Common early People patterns include:

- founder as the centre of all decisions
- roles defined loosely or emotionally
- capability gaps not yet visible
- inconsistent expectations
- team members doing "whatever is needed"
- low clarity on ownership
- heroics masking weak processes
- overvaluing loyalty over capability
- unclear decision rights

Founder psychology distorts this quadrant easily.
Proximity blindness ("I know them well"), narrative attachment ("they were here from the beginning"), and avoidance ("I don't want to have that conversation") blur the true picture.

Key questions:

- Do we have the capability required for the next stage?
- Are roles clear or implied?
- Does decision-making move quickly and cleanly?
- Does the founder carry too much?
- Is the team stable or fatigued?

These reveal your current reality.

POTENTIAL REALITY

A strong People quadrant is coherent, capable and aligned.

Potential looks like:

- clear ownership of outcomes
- decision rights understood across the team
- distributed leadership
- constructive conflict
- high collaboration
- accountability paired with psychological safety
- the right people in the right roles
- capability matched to the next stage, not just the current one
- a team that elevates performance, not depends on the founder

When this state is reached, execution velocity increases dramatically.

THE GAP

The People Gap emerges when the **team you have** is not yet the **team required** for the next stage.

Common Gap patterns:

1. **Role mismatch**
2. People doing jobs not aligned to their strengths.
3. **Leadership bottlenecks**
4. Founder making too many decisions.
5. **Capability gaps**
6. Missing seniority, experience or specialised skill.
7. **Emotional immaturity**
8. Avoidance, reactivity or fragility under pressure.
9. **Communication noise**
10. Information not flowing, misalignment growing.
11. **Team fatigue**
12. Burnout disguised as "busy".
13. **Hiring misaligned to strategy**
14. Reactively filling roles rather than designing roles.

The People Gap often looks "soft," but correcting it often delivers some of the **highest ROI** in the entire Compass.

Expanding capability collapses large Gaps quickly.

FOUNDER PATTERNS

Founders typically fall into one of three instinctive orientations:

1. The Heroic Founder

Carries everything personally.

Strength: pace

Risk: bottlenecks, burnout, dependency

2. The Relational Founder

Warm, loyal, connected.

Strength: cohesion

Risk: avoidance of performance conversations

3. The Systems Founder

Structure-first, clarity-led.

Strength: precision

Risk: underestimating emotional dynamics in teams

Awareness amplifies leadership maturity.

INVESTOR LENS

Investors quietly look for:

- a team that communicates cleanly
- leadership that is self-aware, calm and grounded
- capability matched to stage
- decision quality
- succession risk
- dependency risk
- whether the team amplifies or constrains the founder

Investors know ventures rarely fail because the idea is wrong. They fail because the team cannot execute through complexity.

A strong team builds trust instantly.

QUADRANT INTERACTIONS

People interact with every part of the Compass:

- **Culture** — people shape culture; culture shapes behaviour
- **Structure** — structure enables performance
- **Growth Model** — capability shapes velocity
- **Capital Strategy** — team strength influences investor confidence
- **Validation** — good listeners validate better
- **Integration** — responsible leadership supports responsible growth

The People quadrant is the human engine of the business.

MOVES THAT STRENGTHEN THIS QUADRANT

- clarify roles and expectations
- define decision pathways
- build leadership capacity early
- address capability gaps directly
- coach for emotional maturity
- reduce founder dependency
- establish communication rhythms
- hire strategically, not reactively
- document knowledge
- amplify high-performance behaviours

People become a competitive advantage when they become aligned.

MICRO EXAMPLES

Weak: "We have a great team."

Strong: "Our CTO has shipped two products at this scale, owns the roadmap and is building a team beneath them."

Weak: "Everyone works hard."

Strong: "Each leader owns outcomes with clear metrics and weekly alignment."

MICRO EXERCISE

Role Clarity Prompt

For each team member, answer:

"What outcome do they fully own?"

If you struggle to answer in one sentence, the People Gap is clearer than you think.

A venture becomes scalable when its people become aligned, not only in what they do, but in how they think, decide and communicate.

People are not the heart of the business.

They are the business.

CHAPTER 11

Integration

Every venture interacts with the world around it, socially, culturally, economically and environmentally. The question is not whether the business has an impact, but whether its impact is **coherent**, responsible and aligned with the long-term future the company is trying to create.

In earlier versions of the Compass, this dimension was called "Impact." But the market has evolved. Founders, investors and ecosystems now look beyond impact as a marketing layer or values statement. They look for something deeper and more structural: **Integration**.

Integration asks a different question:
Is the company designed in a way that strengthens the system it depends on?

Not as an ethical flourish.
Not as compliance.
Not as a slide in a pitch deck.

But as a natural result of how the business operates, builds and grows.

Integration is not about perfection.
It is about alignment.

Founder psychology plays a role here. Optimism, narrative inflation and personal attachment to purpose can distort how aligned the business truly is. Integration requires clarity, the structural alignment between intention, behaviour and outcomes.

WHY THIS QUADRANT MATTERS
No venture exists in a vacuum. Every venture operates inside:

- communities
- supply chains
- industries
- markets
- cultures
- regulatory environments
- ecological systems

As the world becomes more interconnected and more constrained, the companies that thrive are the ones designed for coherence between:

- what they deliver
- how they deliver it
- who they affect
- what systems they strengthen
- and what systems they depend on

Integration matters because:

- customers reward alignment
- employees seek meaningful work
- investors manage long-term risk
- regulators reward responsibility
- communities amplify coherence

Integration is not idealism.

It is **strategic stability**.

A company that strengthens its environment reduces risk and increases trust, two of the strongest performance drivers over time.

CURRENT REALITY

In early stages, founders often treat responsibility as a "later" concern. Not out of neglect, but out of survival. As a result:

- good intentions exist, but systems do not
- small misalignments compound
- externalities are unintentionally created
- operations and impact run on separate tracks
- messaging runs ahead of behaviour
- the business grows faster than its responsible design

None of this is unusual.

Integration simply has not been formalised yet.

Key questions:

- Who benefits from our existence and how?
- Who could be harmed and where?
- What system risks do we create?
- Are our intentions reflected in daily operations?
- Are we strengthening or straining key relationships?

These questions bring clarity to current reality.

POTENTIAL REALITY

A coherent, integrated venture looks and behaves differently.

Potential includes:

- clear visibility of system footprint
- alignment between mission and mechanics
- responsible supply chain logic
- transparent communication
- policies that reduce risk
- operational choices that strengthen long-term system health
- a culture that supports responsible behaviour
- value creation that compounds across stakeholders

Integration is not perfection.
Integration is coherence.

THE GAP

The Integration Gap appears when **intention** and **operation** drift apart.

Common patterns:

1. **Intent without implementation**
2. "We care about X," but decisions contradict it.
3. **Growth creating strain**
4. Customer promises outpace capability.
5. **Narrative ahead of behaviour**
6. A strong story without structural follow-through.
7. **System risk ignored**
8. Externalities that later become cost, pressure or complexity.
9. **Misreading stakeholder expectations**
10. Assuming stakeholders care less, or more, than they do.

This Gap often carries high leverage.

When closed, trust, reputation and efficiency increase simultaneously, high ROI across multiple dimensions.

FOUNDER PATTERNS

Three common instincts shape this quadrant:

1. The Idealist

Purpose-led, story-first.

Strength: meaning

Risk: operational drift or not commercial

2. The Operator

Execution-first, impact later.

Strength: delivery

Risk: hidden risk accumulation

3. The Integrator

Sees purpose and operations as one system.

Strength: coherence

Risk: slower decisions if over-analysed

Integration becomes real when intention and behaviour match.

INVESTOR LENS

Investors evaluate Integration through a risk-maturity perspective:

- is the business increasing system stability or strain?
- is there coherence between narrative and practice?

- are externalities accounted for?
- does the company understand stakeholder expectations?
- will future regulation help or harm this model?
- is responsibility built-in or bolted-on?

Integration reduces long-term risk and increases long-term value.

Investors recognise this immediately.

QUADRANT INTERACTIONS

Integration interacts across the Compass:

- **Market Validation** — aligned ventures earn trust faster
- **Market Forces** — cultural and regulatory shifts shape expectations
- **Structure** — responsible design reduces operational risk
- **People** — leadership maturity strengthens alignment
- **Culture** — values expressed through behaviour
- **Capital Strategy** — integrated ventures attract aligned capital

Integration is the coherence layer.

MOVES THAT STRENGTHEN THIS QUADRANT

- make intentions explicit and operational
- identify unintended consequences early
- strengthen supply chain visibility
- align culture with mission
- reduce externalities through design
- create simple responsibility metrics

- communicate clearly, not theatrically
- embed responsibility into growth, not around it

Integration is a design choice.

MICRO EXAMPLES

Weak: "We help the environment."

Strong: "Each unit deployed removes 1.4 tonnes of CO_2 and saves customers 18% annually."

Weak: "We support community wellbeing."

Strong: "Ten percent of our revenue drives direct service delivery to the communities we operate in."

MICRO EXERCISE

Integration Reality Check

Write one line:

"If our company disappeared tomorrow, who would feel it and how?"

If the answer is vague, integration is not yet grounded.

Integration is not an ambition or an initiative.

It is a structural alignment between purpose, behaviour and value.

A company designed with integration at its core becomes more trusted, more resilient and more investable.

CHAPTER 12

The X-Factor

Every venture carries a quality that cannot be captured in metrics alone, a sense of coherence, purpose and internal rhythm that is difficult to measure, hard to imitate and impossible to fake under pressure.

This is the **X-Factor**.

It's the synergy a company produces when its internal and external worlds align, when the hard mechanics and the soft dynamics complement each other, and when the sum of the parts becomes meaningfully greater than the whole.

Most people describe the X-Factor as something they "know when they see it," and in a way that's true. It is a felt sense, an underlying resonance that makes the company feel *inevitable*.

But beneath that mythic quality, the X-Factor is not mysterious.
It is structural.
It is earned.
It is the natural outcome of alignment.

The X-Factor sits at the centre of the Compass because it is shaped by all eight quadrants. It reflects whether the venture's story, structure, culture, people, model and timing have come into a coherent relationship with each other. When they do, the company "feels right" to investors, customers and the team itself.

The X-Factor answers a deeper question:

Does this venture have the internal and external coherence that creates momentum, confidence and inevitability?

When the X-Factor is strong, the company feels clear, focused and grounded.

When it's weak, even strong metrics can feel fragile.

WHY THIS QUADRANT MATTERS

The X-Factor is where the venture's energy and architecture converge.

It is where:

- the narrative matches the numbers
- the numbers match the behaviour
- the behaviour matches the culture
- the culture matches the leadership
- the leadership matches the mission
- and the mission matches the market

This convergence creates *synergy*, the force that makes the business feel bigger, stronger and more capable than the sum of its parts.

A strong X-Factor communicates:

- clarity
- maturity

- stability
- direction
- coherence
- alignment
- focus
- inevitability

A weak X-Factor communicates:
- noise
- doubt
- fragility
- inconsistency

Investors feel this before they analyse it.

Customers sense it before they articulate it.

Teams respond to it before they consciously understand it.

This is why the X-Factor matters, it is the emotional and structural signature of the company.

CURRENT REALITY

In early-stage ventures, the X-Factor is almost always uneven.
Identity, narrative, structure and capability are still forming.

Common patterns include:

- story ahead of execution
- execution ahead of story
- strong product, unclear strategy
- strong team, unclear direction
- internal coherence not yet matching external expression
- founder energy unstable or overstretched

None of this is failure, it is evolution.

The X-Factor emerges as coherence deepens.

POTENTIAL REALITY

A strong X-Factor creates a sense of inevitability.

Potential looks like:

- narrative and numbers reinforcing each other
- strategy matched to stage
- culture matched to pace
- leadership energy steady and grounded
- pricing, product and model aligned
- team speaking in one voice
- the venture knowing what it is and what it is not

In this state, the company develops a kind of internal gravity.

It pulls belief toward it.

It simplifies decisions.

It accelerates conviction.

It reduces noise.

It amplifies resonance.

This is the X-Factor made visible.

THE GAP

The X-Factor Gap appears whenever **internal reality and external expression drift apart**.

Common patterns:
1. **Narrative Inflation**
2. The story stretches beyond the structure.
3. **Narrative Erosion**
4. The story is smaller than the capability.
5. **Identity Drift**
6. The venture evolves but the narrative does not.
7. **Energy Instability**
8. Leadership confidence fluctuates under pressure.
9. **Fragmented Alignment**
10. Different parts of the team are telling different stories.
11. **Strategic Overextension**
12. Too many priorities create confusion, not clarity.

The X-Factor Gap doesn't just signal misalignment; it signals **energetic incoherence**.

Correcting it restores inevitability.

FOUNDER PATTERNS

Founders express the X-Factor through instinctive patterns:

1. The Storyteller

Visionary, charismatic, high narrative strength.

Risk: story ahead of substance.

2. The Operator

Execution-focused, grounded, detail-oriented.

Risk: structure ahead of story.

3. The Integrator

Balances story and structure.

Risk: overthinking alignment during high growth.

Awareness brings stability and coherence.

INVESTOR LENS

Investors don't simply analyse the X-Factor, they **feel** it.

They are looking for:

- coherence
- maturity
- alignment
- grounded momentum
- confidence without bravado
- clarity without inflation
- consistency across team, narrative, structure and numbers

When the X-Factor is strong, conviction forms quickly.

When it is weak, hesitation emerges, even if the metrics look good.

QUADRANT INTERACTIONS

The X-Factor integrates all eight quadrants:

- Validation strengthens the truth of the narrative
- Market Forces shape timing logic
- Growth Model reinforces credibility
- Capital Strategy shapes investor conviction
- Structure stabilises execution
- Culture amplifies trust
- People reinforce capability
- Integration strengthens reputation and responsibility

The X-Factor is not an extra quadrant.

It is the **synergy** created when all quadrants align.

MOVES THAT STRENGTHEN THIS QUADRANT

- simplify the story to its strongest signal
- root the narrative in reality
- ensure internal language matches external expression
- prioritise alignment over speed
- stabilise leadership presence
- correct internal misalignment early
- revisit narrative whenever strategy evolves
- integrate soft and hard systems deliberately

The X-Factor is not charisma.

It is coherence made visible.

MICRO EXAMPLES

Weak: "Our messaging is strong."

Strong: "Our story, numbers and next-stage milestones all reinforce each other."

Weak: "We have a clear roadmap."

Strong: "Our roadmap matches our capacity, capital plan, team capability and model mechanics."

MICRO EXERCISE

Coherence Prompt

Write one sentence:

"Our internal reality and external story align because…"

If you cannot complete this clearly, the X-Factor Gap is active.

THE X-FACTOR IS THE COMPANY'S SIGNATURE

When the story, strategy, structure, culture and behaviour create synergy, the company feels inevitable and that feeling is the X-Factor.

This is the mythic quality founders talk about, the intangible energy investors trust, and the structural alignment that teams respond to instinctively.

When all forces align, the company begins to move with clarity, coherence and gravity.

This is the X-Factor.

CHAPTER 13

The Gap

Every venture lives between two realities; the reality of today and the reality of what is possible. The space between these two states is where growth happens, where capability develops and where the true work of building a business takes place.

This space is **the Gap**.

The Gap is not a flaw, not a failing, not a deficiency.
It is the structural distance between **current reality** and **potential reality** across each quadrant of the Compass.

The most successful founders are not the ones with the smallest Gaps.
They are the ones who understand their Gaps accurately and move through them deliberately.

The Gap is the engine of transformation, the foundation of sequencing and, as we will outline, the basis of the venture's **investment logic**.

The Gap and Return on Investment
The Gap is not only a diagnostic.
It is the foundation of the ROI logic behind every strategic move and every investment decision.

The cost of closing the Gap, in capital, time and capability, represents the investment required to move from where the business is to where it could be.

Investors, founders and shareholders all evaluate:
- What is the Gap?
- What will it cost to close?
- What capability or capital is needed?
- What is the expected return if we bridge it?
- What is the risk if we don't?

A clear Gap makes investment decisions coherent.
A distorted Gap misprices the journey.

This is why the psychological layer matters.
Fear, overconfidence and optimism bias distort how founders see:
- their current reality,
- their potential reality,
- the size of the Gap,
- and the cost to close it.

The Compass brings structure and objectivity.
It clarifies the Gap so founders and investors can see the same distance with the same degree of accuracy.

CURRENT REALITY → POTENTIAL REALITY
Across each quadrant, Validation, Market Forces, Growth, Capital, Structure, People, Culture, Integration, there is a current state and a potential state.

The Gap is the **distance** between them.

Examples:

- Early traction exists (current), but behaviour is not repeatable (potential).
- Strong product exists (current), but pricing is misaligned (potential).
- Capable team exists (current), but leadership maturity is fragmented (potential).
- Vision is strong (current), but the narrative does not match the numbers (potential).

The Gap gives founders a precise language for what needs to shift, without emotion, without confusion.

CATEGORIES OF GAPS (MAPPED TO THE COMPASS)

Grouping the most common Gaps under the eight quadrants brings clarity:

1. Market Validation Gaps

- Interest without behaviour
- Conversion without retention
- Retention without advocacy
- Undefined segment
- Evidence mismatch between narrative and traction

2. Market Forces Gaps

- Misread timing
- Overstated market size

- Ignoring structural constraints
- Underestimating incumbents
- External risk unaccounted for

3. Growth Model Gaps

- Founder-led revenue
- Low activation
- High churn
- No repeatability
- Pricing misaligned with economics

4. Capital Strategy Gaps

- Wrong type of capital
- Misaligned investor expectations
- Unclear milestone logic
- Raising too early or too late
- Underestimating capital intensity

5. Structure Gaps

- Margin instability
- Weak governance
- Role ambiguity
- Process fragility
- Operational bottlenecks

6. Culture Gaps

- Avoidance of difficult conversations
- Values not evidenced by behaviour

- Low trust
- Psychological safety instability
- Leadership tone inconsistency

7. People Gaps

- Missing capability for next stage
- Founder bottlenecks
- Misplaced roles
- Weak decision pathways
- Fatigue / burnout

8. Integration Gaps

- Purpose unreconciled with operations
- Externalities ignored
- Responsibility misaligned
- Narrative ahead of behaviour
- Misunderstood stakeholder impact

These are the structural Gaps.

But there is one more category that founders often overlook, the foundational layer.

FOUNDATIONAL GAPS (BENEATH THE COMPASS)

These are behavioural, psychological and decision-making patterns that influence every quadrant:

- optimism bias
- overconfidence

- proximity blindness

- narrative attachment

- equating effort with progress

- fear of seeing the truth

- anchoring in an outdated story

- founder exceptionalism ("this doesn't apply to us")

- avoidance of the hardest or most painful Gap

These Gaps distort the rest of the Compass.

This is why Chapter 14 exists, to bring accuracy back into the assessment.

GAP SEVERITY AND EFFORT TO CLOSE

Not all Gaps are equal.

Some look large but are easy to close.

Others look small but are expensive in time, energy or capability.

Two dimensions reveal the true shape of the Gap:

Gap Severity

How much the Gap affects momentum and coherence.

Low / Medium / High

Effort to Close

How much cost, capability or capital is required.

Low / Medium / High

This produces **four gap types**:

1. High Impact / Low Effort
The fastest wins, often hidden in plain sight.

Examples:

- tightening the segment
- adjusting onboarding
- clarifying ownership
- refining the narrative
- improving communication rhythm

2. High Impact / High Effort
The ones that shape funding strategy and sequencing.

Examples:

- rebuilding the pricing architecture
- senior leadership hire
- complete model redesign
- major structural shifts

3. Low Impact / Low Effort
Quick clean-up.

Examples:

- tightening reporting cadence
- simplifying internal tools
- updating contracts

4. Low Impact / High Effort

Avoid early, low ROI until the business is mature.

Examples:

- heavy process automation
- complex partnerships
- full brand repositioning too early

Dangers of Mis-scoring the Gap

Founders typically distort the Gap in two ways:

1. Overstretching the Gap

- Vision inflated
- Potential overstated
- Timeline unrealistic
- Capital need underestimated
- Capability overestimated

This creates pressure, failure loops and mistrust.

2. Understretching the Gap

- Playing too small
- Avoiding structural changes
- Under-investing in capability
- Under-sequencing growth
- Seeing growth as "incremental" rather than transformational

This creates stagnation and missed opportunity.

The Compass stabilises both distortions.

INVESTOR LENS ON THE GAP

Investors quietly ask:

- Is the Gap real?
- Is it grounded in evidence?
- Is the cost to close understood?
- Is the team capable of bridging it?
- Is the sequence correct?
- Is the expected ROI credible?

Investors invest in **Gap closure**, not noise.

A founder who understands their Gap creates confidence.
A founder who distorts their Gap creates hesitation.

MICRO EXAMPLES (GAP-RELATED)

Weak: "We're almost ready to scale."
Strong: "Retention is at 42%, activation is inconsistent, and pricing is unstable, scaling now would increase burn."

Weak: "We could triple revenue next year."
Strong: "We could triple revenue if we close the churn Gap and complete two capability hires."

MICRO EXERCISES (LIGHTWEIGHT PROMPTS)

1. Gap Clarity Exercise

For each gap, write:

- Severity: Low / Medium / High
- Effort: Low / Medium / High

This instantly reveals where to focus.

2. Quick-Win Finder

List 3 Gaps that are High Impact / Low Effort.
These are your fastest leverage points.

3. ROI Thinking Prompt

Write one sentence:

"What return would closing this Gap create for the business?"

This shifts thinking from symptom to strategy.

The Gap Is the Journey

Every venture begins in one reality
and grows toward another.

The Gap is the space between.
It is the work.
It is the opportunity.
It is the investment logic
and the pathway
and the map of transformation.

The Compass shows the map.
The Gap shows the path.

PART III — APPLYING THE COMPASS

Chapters 14–20

CHAPTER 14

Reading Your Own Venture
Through the Compass

The Venture Compass is not just a framework. It is a lens, a way of seeing your business with more clarity, precision and honesty than the day-to-day rhythm usually allows. The power of the Compass emerges when founders use it to examine their own venture without defensiveness, without assumption and without fear of what they might find.

The goal is simple:

to see the truth of the business as it is today, so you can move it toward what it is capable of becoming.

Founders rarely pause long enough to do this. The pace of building, selling, leading and raising capital creates a constant forward motion that leaves little space for reflection. But clarity does not come from speed. It comes from perspective.

This chapter gives you a structured, practical way to read your own venture through the Compass and identify the patterns that matter most.

THE DISTORTION LAYER: WHY FOUNDERS MISREAD THEIR OWN VENTURES

Before entering the structured assessment, it is important to recognise what sits beneath every founder's self-assessment: **fear, bias and emotional distortion.**

These forces do not come from weakness.
They come from being human.

But when unacknowledged, they distort the truth, especially the **shape, size and cost of the Gap**.

Fear-Based Distortion

Fear often shows up as:

- overstating traction
- understating risk
- avoiding weak areas
- inflating market size
- defending insecure parts of the business
- resisting uncomfortable evidence

Fear narrows perception.
The Compass widens it.

Cognitive Biases

Founders are especially prone to:

- **optimism bias** — believing outcomes will be better than evidence suggests

- **overconfidence** — assuming capability will appear because it is intended
- **proximity blindness** — being too close to see what is obvious to others
- **narrative attachment** — holding onto the origin story too tightly
- **sunk cost fallacy** — keeping strategies alive because they were expensive
- **founder exceptionalism** — "this won't apply to us because..."

These biases distort the Gap.

They make it look too small, too large, too easy or too impossible.

Emotional Attachment

Many founders unintentionally equate:

- the business with their identity
- traction with worth
- setbacks with failure
- criticism with threat

This emotional entanglement blurs the ability to see reality objectively.

The Compass exists to override this distortion.

It creates distance, enough space for structural clarity to emerge.

Fear and bias distort the picture.

The Compass gives you the structure to override that distortion.

A light reference for those wanting deeper work:

The psychological patterns and inner journey behind these distortions are explored more fully in the book *The Hero's Journey – Insights from a Serial Entrepreneur by Mark Falzon (available on Kindle)* not required reading, simply context.

THE THREE-LAYER VIEW

When reading your venture through the Compass, look through three layers:

1. The Observable Layer

Facts, data, behaviour.

- revenue
- churn
- acquisition cost
- retention
- team size
- unit economics
- onboarding behaviour
- customer activation

2. The Interpretive Layer

Meaning beneath the metrics.

- why customers behave the way they do
- what friction points reveal
- what numbers hide
- where execution feels heavy

- what the team avoids
- where decisions stall

3. The Integrative Layer

Coherence across the system.

- does the story match the numbers?
- does the team match the mission?
- does the model match the market?
- does the culture match the pace?
- does the structure match the ambition?
- does the leadership match the moment?

A strong Compass reading integrates all three.

Start with Curiosity, Not Judgment

When founders self-diagnose, they fall into two traps:

The Defensive Trap

"I already know what's wrong."

(Usually a surface-level interpretation masking deeper patterns.)

The Harsh Trap

"We're behind. We're failing."

(Emotional interpretation rather than structural insight.)

The goal is neither self-protection nor self-critique.

The goal is **clarity**.

Curiosity dissolves distortion.

A STRUCTURED WAY TO SELF-ASSESS

Use this seven-step approach:

Step 1: Assess each quadrant independently

Don't let strong areas hide weak ones.

Step 2: Identify strengths first

Strengths anchor momentum.

Step 3: Name the single biggest constraint in each quadrant

Not a list, the constraint.

Step 4: Look for cross-quadrant patterns

This is where the real truth emerges.

Step 5: State your current reality clearly

Simple, honest language removes emotional noise.

Step 6: Describe your potential reality

What is truly possible if constraints are resolved?

Step 7: Map the Gap

This is the structural distance between the two, the foundation of sequencing and ROI.

HOW PSYCHOLOGY DISTORTS THE GAP

This part belongs explicitly here:

Overstretching the Gap

- unrealistic potential
- inflated timelines
- underestimated cost
- overestimated capability

Understretching the Gap

- conservative ambition
- avoiding necessary change
- under-investing in capability
- misreading potential

Mispricing the Gap

- the cost of capability is unclear
- the capital required is underestimated
- the ROI logic is distorted
- the investment case becomes unstable

The Compass stabilises all three distortions.

MICRO EXAMPLES

Weak: "We're nearly ready to raise."

Strong: "We lack retention consistency, a clear pricing architecture and a senior technical hire, raising now would create pressure, not progress."

Weak: "Our team is strong."

Strong: "Execution depends on two people; we need clearer ownership and decision rights."

MICRO EXERCISES (LIGHT, QUICK)

Perspective Exercise

Write the story you tell yourself about your weakest area.

Then write the evidence.

The gap between the two is where distortion lives.

Blind Spot Exercise

Ask one trusted team member:

"What's the one thing we avoid talking about?"

That is often the true Gap.

Gap Grounding Exercise

For your biggest constraint, write two lines:

- What it costs the business today
- What closing it would create in value

This ties psychology back to ROI.

The Power of Seeing Clearly

When founders use the Compass honestly, clarity emerges quickly:

- the venture is stronger than expected,

  or

- the constraints are clearer than expected,

  or

- one or two big moves change everything,

  or

- the Gap is wide, but the path is clear.

What changes is not the business —
what changes is what the founder can see.

You stop asking:
"What is wrong?"
and start asking:
"What is the next structural move that creates progress?"

This is where leadership matures.

The Compass as a Practice
A single reading is valuable.
A regular rhythm transforms.

- use the Compass quarterly
- revisit it after strategic shifts
- check it before fundraising
- use it to align your team around priorities
- use it when the business feels heavy or unclear

Clarity compounds.
Self-awareness compounds.
Alignment compounds.

The Compass brings all three.

CHAPTER 15

Understanding Your Gap Profile

Every venture has a Gap, not as a flaw, but as a structural truth.

But not all Gaps behave the same way. Some stretch cleanly. Some constrain progress. Some appear large but are easy to close. Some appear small but are expensive, slow or capability-intensive. Understanding your **Gap Profile** gives you clarity on how your structural Gaps interact and what kind of movement is required to close them.

A Gap Profile is simply the pattern of Gaps across the Compass.

Once you understand your profile, you gain three advantages:

- **Clarity** about what type of company you are right now
- **Confidence** about the path forward
- **Calm** because the Gap becomes structural, not emotional

The key is to see your Gap Profile **accurately**, without distortion from optimism, fear, overconfidence or narrative attachment. Founder psychology can stretch or shrink the Gap in ways that don't reflect reality. The Compass stabilises this.

THE FOUR PRIMARY GAP PROFILES

Across hundreds of ventures, four dominant profiles appear. Most ventures are a blend, but one usually leads.

1. THE EARLY SIGNAL PROFILE

(The venture has promise, but not yet pattern)

This appears when signals are positive but inconsistent.

Indicators:

- early traction without repeatability
- interest without clear behaviour
- narrative ahead of mechanics
- founder effort driving results
- unstable or unclear activation patterns

Founder distortion risk: **overstating early momentum.**
What's needed:
stronger validation, clearer mechanics, structural clarity.

This is not a weakness, it is a formation stage.

2. THE STRONG BUT FRAGMENTED PROFILE

(The venture has strengths, but alignment is missing)

Indicators:

- strong product, weak story
- strong culture, weak structure
- strong founder, stretched team
- strong revenue, unstable margins
- strong narrative, unclear economics

Founder distortion risk: **ignoring structural misalignment** because parts of the business look good.

What's needed:
coherence, narrative, strategy, model and team alignment.

This profile has enormous upside once aligned.

3. THE OVERSTRETCHED PROFILE

(The venture is growing, but the foundation is struggling)

Indicators:

- rising revenue with rising chaos
- systems breaking under load
- team fatigue
- decision bottlenecks
- delivery quality slipping
- founder over-extension

Founder distortion risk: **confusing speed with scalability**.

What's needed:
stabilisation, structure, people, pricing and rhythm.

This profile has momentum but requires consolidation.

4. THE MISALIGNED PROFILE

(The story, model or behaviour doesn't match reality)

Indicators:

- strong pitch, weak mechanics
- inconsistent execution
- unclear direction across the team
- narrative behind the strategy
- founder energy mismatched to stage
- internal and external reality not synced

Founder distortion risk:

story inflation or story erosion, both distort the Gap.

What's needed:

re-grounding, clarity, cohesion and narrative alignment.

This profile is highly correctable when named early.

HOW TO IDENTIFY YOUR GAP PROFILE

Three simple questions reveal your profile:

1. Where is the friction?

Where do things feel heavy, slow or noisy?

2. Where is the leakage?

Where is value, time, margin or energy being lost?

3. Where is the tension?

Where does your current behaviour not match your intended direction?

Patterns always reveal the truth.

WHAT YOUR GAP PROFILE DOES NOT MEAN

Your profile is **not**:

- a judgment
- a grade
- a prediction
- a label
- a weakness

It is simply the structural truth of where you are.

Every high-performing venture moves through all four profiles at some point.

What matters is not the profile but the **movement**.

GAP SEVERITY AND EFFORT TO CLOSE

Your Gap Profile becomes more actionable when paired with two simple lenses:

Gap Severity:

Low / Medium / High — the impact of the Gap on momentum.

Effort to Close:

Low / Medium / High — the capital, capability or time required.

Combined, they create four Gap types:

- **High impact / Low effort** — fastest wins
- **High impact / High effort** — shape capital strategy

- **Low impact / Low effort** — quick cleanups
- **Low impact / High effort** — defer unless strategically necessary

This lens helps founders avoid distortion, not overstretching the Gap, and not under stretching it.

MICRO EXAMPLES

Weak: "We're almost ready to scale."
Strong: "We lack a stable pricing model and predictable retention, scaling now increases burn."

Weak: "Our team is strong."
Strong: "Two critical roles don't have clear ownership, we need to close that Gap before adding complexity."

MICRO EXERCISE

Gap Profile Prompt
Write the one-sentence truth for each quadrant:
"Our current reality is X, our potential reality is Y."

This immediately reveals:
- your pattern
- your profile
- your true priority
- your blind spots
- and your next structural move

USING YOUR GAP PROFILE TO CREATE MOVEMENT

Once you know your profile, the next step becomes clear:

Early Signal → strengthen validation and mechanics

Strong but Fragmented → align narrative, model, team and structure

Overstretched → stabilise operational foundations

Misaligned → restore coherence across story, model and behaviour

The Shift begins with naming the truth.
Movement begins with the right next step.

Your Gap Profile tells you not only where you are —
but **what type of movement the moment requires.**

CHAPTER 16

Upgrading Your Venture Using Compass Logic

Clarity is powerful but clarity alone does not create progress.

Progress comes from movement: intentional, sequenced, leverage-driven movement that shifts the business from its current reality toward its potential reality.

The Venture Compass is not just a diagnostic.

It is an operating system for transformation.

Once you understand your Gaps, the real work begins: knowing which moves matter most, when to make them and how to avoid the common traps founders fall into.

The goal is not to fix everything.

The goal is to make the **one move** that changes everything else.

THE PRINCIPLE OF LEVERAGE

High-performing founders do not do more.

They do the right things in the right sequence.

Compass logic is built on a single principle:

Identify the smallest structural move that creates the greatest shift across the system.

This principle prevents the three most common errors:

1. Overstretching

Trying to close too many Gaps at once, driven by urgency or optimism bias.

2. Understretching

Avoiding necessary upgrades because they feel uncomfortable or capability-intensive.

3. Misprioritising

Choosing work that feels easy over work that creates real movement.

Leverage is the antidote to all three.

THE FIVE CORE MOVES

Every venture upgrades through a pattern of structural moves. These moves correspond directly to the types of Gaps identified in the Compass.

MOVE 1: CLARIFY THE SIGNAL

Strengthens **Market Validation**.

Shifts growth from push to pull.

This includes:

- tightening the segment
- refining messaging
- measuring behaviour, not interest
- clarifying activation
- reducing friction in the buying journey

MOVE 2: STRENGTHEN THE ENGINE

Strengthens the **Growth Model**.

This includes:

- reducing churn
- tuning pricing
- improving activation
- building repeatability
- validating channels
- stabilising unit economics

A clean engine reduces capital intensity dramatically.

MOVE 3: REINFORCE THE FRAME

Stabilises **Structure**.

This includes:

- tightening margins
- clarifying decision rights
- documenting processes
- strengthening governance
- establishing operating rhythms

This move often collapses multiple Gaps simultaneously.

MOVE 4: ELEVATE THE TEAM

Strengthens **People** and **Culture**.

This includes:

- capability upgrades
- decision pathway clarity
- reducing founder dependency
- addressing performance gaps
- creating communication rhythms

Team maturity increases velocity.

MOVE 5: REALIGN THE STORY

Strengthens the **X-Factor**.

This includes:

- simplifying the narrative
- aligning story and numbers
- updating messaging after structural changes
- ensuring the team speaks with one voice

Coherence accelerates investor confidence.

HOW TO CHOOSE THE RIGHT MOVE

Once you understand your Gap Profile, the "next move" becomes clear:

Early Signal Profile → Clarify the Signal (Move 1)

Strong but Fragmented Profile → Realign the Story + Reinforce the Frame (Moves 5 + 3)

Overstretched Profile → Reinforce the Frame + Elevate the Team (Moves 3 + 4)

Misaligned Profile → Realign the Story + targeted structural moves (Moves 5 + others)

Do not push all five moves at once.
Start with the one that has the highest leverage.

THE POWER OF SEQUENCING

Sequencing is often more important than speed.

Examples:

- fixing structure before validation wastes time
- scaling acquisition before retention increases burn
- raising capital before model stability increases pressure
- refining narrative before execution improves creates distrust
- hiring without clarity increases noise

A simple rule:

Fix the bottom of the funnel before the top.
Fix stability before scale.

Correct sequencing turns effort into momentum.
Incorrect sequencing turns effort into noise.

THE GAP AND ROI

Every strategic move can be understood through a simple lens:

Does this move close the Gap in a way that creates meaningful ROI?

This includes:

- efficiency
- margin
- execution speed
- capital leverage
- capability uplift
- market readiness

High-ROI moves change the shape of the venture.
Low-ROI moves keep the venture busy.

The Compass helps founders avoid the distortion that leads to miscalculation:

- overstretching (inflating potential, underestimating cost)
- under stretching (playing too small)
- mispricing the Gap (misaligning capital, capability or time)

The roadmap corrects this and creates grounded, investable sequence.

THE 12-WEEK TRANSFORMATION MODEL

The most effective transformation cycles run in 12-week blocks.

Weeks 1–2

Diagnose the Gap

Choose the leverage move

Define milestones and metrics

Weeks 3–10

Execute

Remove obstacles

Strengthen the relevant quadrant

Communicate progress

Weeks 11–12

Measure outcomes

Integrate learnings

Reassess the Compass

Set the next cycle

This rhythm builds compounding clarity.

MICRO EXAMPLES

Weak: "Our next 90 days are about growth."

Strong: "Our next 90 days are about stabilising onboarding to stop losing customers we're already winning."

Weak: "We're focusing on product."

Strong: "We're closing the activation Gap by refining our core value moment."

MICRO EXERCISE

Leverage Finder

List your top three constraints.

For each, write:

Impact: Low / Medium / High

Effort to Close: Low / Medium / High

The move you want is:

High Impact × Low Effort.

Begin there.

THE VENTURE BEGINS TO FEEL DIFFERENT

As founders use Compass logic:

- tension decreases
- clarity increases
- execution stabilises
- culture strengthens
- team alignment improves
- investor conversations become cleaner
- decisions feel calmer
- the X-Factor strengthens

This is the compounding effect of structure, clarity and coherence.

The roadmap does not push the venture harder.

It aligns the venture more intelligently.

The Compass shows the map.
The roadmap creates the movement.

CHAPTER 17

The Venture Compass Free Assessment

One of the most common questions founders ask after first encountering the Compass is simple:

"Where do we begin?"

The Venture Compass Free Assessment exists to give founders an immediate first look at their business through the Compass lens, without complexity, without overwhelm and without needing to interpret all nine forces on their own.

It provides a **quick, structured snapshot** of how the venture presents today across the core forces of the Compass. It is not a full diagnostic, and it is not designed to replace deep analysis. It is a clear, early signal, the first read before the real work begins.

Founders often overestimate or underestimate their current reality because of fear, optimism bias or narrative attachment. The Free Assessment helps override that distortion and grounds the founder in an objective starting point.

WHAT THE FREE ASSESSMENT MEASURES
The scan provides light-touch insight across the Compass:
- Market Validation
- Market Forces

- Growth Model

- Capital Strategy

- Structure

- Culture

- People

- Integration

Each dimension includes:

- a simple star rating

- a concise insight

- one or two priority cues

These ratings are not definitive judgments.

They are signals, early markers of how the business presents externally.

Psychological proximity often distorts internal judgment.

The Free Assessment acts as an external mirror.

WHAT THE FREE ASSESSMENT DOES NOT DO

The Free Assessment is intentionally simple. It does **not** attempt to:

- diagnose the full Gap

- interpret cross-quadrant patterns

- analyse economics or model stability

- assess capability or leadership maturity

- map structural risks

- evaluate ROI or capital sequencing

These belong to the **full Compass Report**, which goes significantly deeper.

The Free Assessment's purpose is orientation, not diagnosis.

THE VALUE OF A FIRST READ

Founders frequently discover unexpected insights:

- an assumed strength might show as average
- a perceived weakness might be less consequential than believed
- early traction patterns may be clearer than expected
- blind spots become visible
- the "story" and the "reality" may diverge

The value lies in **seeing the starting point clearly**.
You cannot navigate without knowing where you are.

THE GAP → ROI LINK (Light and Clean)

While the Free Assessment does not calculate investment logic,
it provides the **first signals** that shape it.

A founder's ability to close the Gap between current and potential reality
depends on:

- capability
- capital
- time
- sequence

The Free Assessment reveals which quadrants may eventually require deeper investment and which offer early wins.

It prepares the ground for the deeper ROI lens that appears in the full report.

HOW TO ACCESS THE FREE ASSESSMENT

Throughout this book, you'll find links directing you to the most current version of the Venture Compass Free Assessment.

Tools evolve.

Platforms improve.

The link ensures you always receive the latest version.

www.theventurecompass.com

MICRO EXAMPLE

Weak: "We think we're strong across most quadrants."

Strong: "The Free Assessment shows two stable quadrants and four that need deeper analysis, especially pricing and retention."

MICRO EXERCISE

Free Assessment Reflection Prompt

After completing the scan, write one line:

"The quadrant that surprised me most was…"

Surprise reveals distortion and points to the real Gap.

THE ROLE OF THE FREE ASSESSMENT IN THE FOUNDER JOURNEY

The Free Assessment is not the full Compass.

It is the **first signal**, the orientation point, the beginning of a clearer conversation with yourself, your team and your investors.

Founders who begin here gain immediate awareness of where they stand and where deeper structural work may be needed.

The deeper insights come later.

The first step is simply seeing clearly.

The Free Assessment gives you that step.

CHAPTER 18

The Full Venture Compass Report

The Venture Compass Free Assessment gives founders an early glimpse of how their venture presents across the quadrants. But a snapshot is not a diagnosis. Early signals rarely reveal the full shape of a company's strengths, risks or growth potential.

The **Full Venture Compass Report** exists to provide a deeper, more structured interpretation, the kind of analysis founders rarely receive, and the kind of insight investors rely on to make decisions. It illuminates what sits *beneath* the surface, not just what is visible at a glance.

This report translates your venture into a multi-dimensional assessment that helps you understand what is working, what is weak, what is misaligned and what needs to shift next.

It is not prescriptive.
It is clarifying.

And for both founders and investors, clarity is the starting point of intelligent movement.

WHY THE FULL REPORT MATTERS

Founders operate from the inside of the business, immersed in decisions, details, fire-fighting and momentum. This internal view is essential, but it also creates blind spots.

The full report provides an **external, pattern-based, structural view**. It reveals:

- the truth beneath surface-level traction
- misalignments hidden by founder optimism or urgency
- structural weaknesses that could collapse under scale
- strengths the founder may be underestimating
- patterns that shape future performance
- the shape and cost of the Gap
- the most logical sequencing for progress
- the clearest ROI pathways

A founder cannot correct a Gap they cannot see.
The full report shows the Gap accurately, without distortion from fear, hope or bias.

WHAT THE FULL REPORT INCLUDES

1. Executive Summary

A clear overview of strengths, risks, patterns and trajectory across the nine forces.

2. Quadrant-by-Quadrant Assessment

Each quadrant receives a concise analysis interpreting:

- behavioural signals
- model logic

- economics and mechanics
- leadership and culture patterns
- structural readiness
- alignment or misalignment with stage

3. Cross-Pattern Reading

This is where the deepest insight is found.

The report examines interactions between quadrants:

- validation + retention
- timing + category dynamics
- pricing + margin stability
- team + execution velocity
- narrative + X-Factor coherence
- structure + capital strategy
- culture + execution quality

These interactions reveal the forces shaping the trajectory.

4. Risk Table

Not as prediction but as pattern-recognition.

5. Opportunities and Upside

Where small shifts can create large movement.

6. 30 / 60 / 90 Day Roadmap

A focused sequence that turns diagnostic clarity into momentum.

7. Optional Narrative Summary

A refined articulation of the venture's story based on structural truth, not pitch polish.

THE GAP & ROI LOGIC (LIGHT ADDITION)

One of the most valuable elements of the full report is the clarity it brings to the **Gap** and therefore to investment logic.

The cost to close the Gap (in capability, capital and time) is the **true investment required** for the company to reach its potential. Investors, founders and boards need an accurate picture of:

- the size of the Gap
- the effort to close it
- the capital required
- the expected return
- the sequencing needed
- the risks of not closing it

Distorted Gaps lead to distorted investment plans.
Clear Gaps lead to grounded, credible, investable plans.

The report removes distortion.

WHAT THE FULL REPORT DOES NOT DO

It does not:

- replace leadership judgment
- tell you what to do
- create heavy frameworks
- predict outcomes

- solve capability gaps
- override your context
- act as a performance review

It is a **structural read**, not a prescription.

Its power lies in clarity, not instruction.

HOW FOUNDERS USE THE FULL REPORT

Founders typically leverage the full report in four ways:

1. Clarifying Priorities

Identifying the highest-leverage Gap.

2. Refining the Narrative

Ensuring the story matches the structure.

3. Improving Investor Readiness

Building grounded conviction through clarity.

4. Aligning the Team

Creating shared understanding across leadership.

When everyone sees the same reality, execution becomes cleaner.

MICRO EXAMPLES

Weak: "We're strong in most areas."

Strong: "Our Compass report shows validation and culture are stable, but pricing and retention need priority."

Weak: "We know our weaknesses."
Strong: "Our biggest Gap is the churn + onboarding interaction, that's what we're closing next."

MICRO EXERCISE
Full Report Reflection Prompt
Write down the **one Insight** from the full report that surprised you most.
Then write the **one move** that flows directly from it.

Surprise reveals blind spots.
Movement begins there.

HOW TO ACCESS THE FULL REPORT
Like the Free Assessment, the Full Report is available through a simple pathway.
To maintain quality and accuracy, tools evolve.
Use the link to access the most current version.
www.theventurecompass.com

CLARITY THAT LEADS TO MOVEMENT
The Full Compass Report is not designed to overwhelm.
It is designed to illuminate.

It gives founders a precise read of reality —
without distortion, without judgement and without confusion.

Once you can see the truth,
the next moves become obvious.

The Compass shows the map.
The Full Report reveals the terrain.

CHAPTER 19

From Report to Roadmap:
Prioritising the Right Moves

A Venture Compass report, whether the free snapshot or the full diagnostic, gives you clarity. But clarity alone does not create progress. Progress comes from knowing *what to do with that clarity*, and from choosing the right moves in a sequence that strengthens the venture without overwhelming it.

The roadmap is where insight becomes movement.
It shows how to close the Gap between current reality and potential reality with precision, structure and intention.

The goal is not to fix everything.
The goal is to make the **smallest structural move that creates the greatest shift across the system.**

THE SHIFT FROM DIAGNOSIS TO MOVEMENT
A diagnosis reveals the state of the system.
A roadmap reshapes the system.

This transition requires a shift in mindset:
- from reacting emotionally → to acting structurally
- from trying to fix everything → to identifying leverage

- from broad effort $\rightarrow$ to narrow precision
- from founder heroics $\rightarrow$ to capability-led execution
- from narrative $\rightarrow$ to sequence

The first task after reviewing your Compass results is not to create a list of actions.

It is to choose the **one move** that matters most.

A single, well-sequenced decision will shift more than fifty small ones.

THE RULE OF ONE

Founders often overreact to a diagnostic by attempting to solve too much at once. This creates noise, fragmentation and slow progress.

Compass logic demands the opposite:

Start with one move, the move with the highest combined score of Gap Severity × Effort to Close (low).

This prevents overwhelm and accelerates momentum.

THE THREE-STEP PRIORITISATION MODEL

Step 1: Identify the Highest-Leverage Quadrant

Ask:

"Which quadrant is holding the business back the most?"

Not the quadrant that feels dramatic.

The quadrant that contains the **root constraint**.

Step 2: Name the Single Most Important Move

Examples:

- Market Validation → tighten the segment
- Growth Model → reduce churn
- Capital Strategy → refine milestone logic
- Structure → rebuild pricing
- People → clarify roles
- Culture → create a communication rhythm
- Integration → align operations with intention
- X-Factor → simplify the narrative

The move should be small, precise and structural.

Step 3: Build a 30–60–90 Day Plan

Your next three months should flow like this:

30 Days — Stabilise

Clarify, reset or rebuild the foundations required for the move.

60 Days — Strengthen

Implement, refine and embed improvements.

90 Days — Scale

Extend the improvement into other functions and measure its effect.

This creates a rhythm the business can sustain.

The Gap and ROI

A roadmap is not just an operational plan.

It is an investment sequence.

Each move in the roadmap is chosen because it increases:

- structural stability,
- commercial viability,
- team capability,
- and return on capital.

Investors, founders and boards all evaluate the venture through a simple lens:

Does this roadmap close the Gap in a way that creates meaningful ROI?

Large-sounding problems are often low effort to solve.
Small-sounding issues can be expensive.
A roadmap makes this distinction clear.

GAP DISTORTION AND ROADMAP ERRORS
Founder bias and emotional distortion can derail the roadmap:

Overstretching

- too much ambition
- unrealistic timelines
- raising before readiness
- building ahead of validation

Understretching

- playing small
- avoiding mission-critical upgrades
- undercapitalising
- delaying hard structural work

Misprioritising

- tackling high-effort / low-impact items first
- avoiding high-impact / low-effort gains
- letting fear or preference pick priorities

The Compass stabilises these distortions by grounding the roadmap in structural truth.

MICRO EXAMPLES

Weak: "We need to grow faster."

Strong: "We need to close our retention Gap so growth creates margin, not burn."

Weak: "Our next 90 days are about sales."

Strong: "Our next 90 days are about stabilising onboarding to stop losing the customers we're already winning."

MICRO EXERCISE (LIGHT, FOUNDER-FRIENDLY)

Leverage Finder

List three constraints surfaced in your report.

For each, write:

Impact: Low / Medium / High

Effort to Close: Low / Medium / High

Choose the move that is:

High Impact × Low Effort.

Start there.

What Happens When the Roadmap Is Structured Well

Founders often notice a distinct shift as the roadmap takes hold:

- tension decreases
- clarity increases
- team energy stabilises
- decisions become simpler
- execution becomes cleaner
- investor conversations improve
- the X-Factor strengthens

This shift is not accidental.
It is the compounding effect of structure, sequence and clarity.

A roadmap built on Compass logic does not push the venture harder.
It aligns the venture more coherently.

Closing the Gap becomes a predictable, achievable sequence, not an emotional struggle.

The Compass shows the map.

The roadmap creates the movement.

PART IV — BEYOND THE BOOK

Chapters 21–23 + Further Exploration + Afterword

CHAPTER 20

What Investors Actually See

Investors sit in a world founders rarely get to observe. Not because the world is secretive, but because assessment, pattern-recognition and risk evaluation happen behind closed doors, in conversations founders never hear and in frames founders are not trained to see.

The result is a quiet asymmetry:
Founders pitch with emotion. Investors evaluate with structure.

Founders experience pressure, urgency, hope and fear.
Investors assess patterns, readiness, risk and ROI.

This chapter removes the mystery.
Not to teach founders how to "pitch better," but to help them see their venture through the same structural lens investors use, the lens that turns clarity into conviction.

THE INVESTOR VIEW IS STRUCTURAL, NOT PERSONAL
Founders hear *yes*, *no* and *silence*.

Investors see:

- pattern alignment
- risk concentration

- Gap accuracy
- capability maturity
- timing and market conditions
- capital efficiency
- model logic
- sequencing
- ROI (explicit and implicit)

Investors are not evaluating the founder's worth, character or intent.

They are evaluating the **structure** of the venture:

its trajectory, its risks, its potential and what it will take to close the Gap.

The decision is structural, not emotional.

THE THREE QUESTIONS INVESTORS ARE ALWAYS ASKING

Beneath every meeting, every deck and every reference check, investors are assessing:

1. "Is there something real here?"

Market Validation, Market Forces, Capital Strategy

2. "Is this structurally ready to grow?"

Growth Model, Structure, People, Integrated

3. "Is this the team that can do it?"

Culture, X-Factor.

When these three answer "yes," momentum builds.

When one is unclear, conviction weakens.

THE GAP → ROI LOGIC (LIGHT, CRITICAL)

Investors think in terms of **Gap closure**:

"What is the Gap, what does it cost to close, and what return will it generate?"

They assess:

- the size of the Gap
- the cost (capital + capability + time)
- the feasibility of closing it
- the sequence required
- the team's maturity
- the risk-adjusted return

Founders often distort the Gap because of hope, fear or narrative attachment. Investors cannot rely on emotional interpretation, they need structural clarity.

The Compass aligns both sides around the same truth.

PATTERN-BASED DECISION-MAKING

Investors compare your venture against:

- every company they've ever evaluated
- every founder they've backed
- every failure pattern they've seen
- every successful trajectory
- every early warning sign

- every structural Gap that once looked small but wasn't
- every model that scaled cleanly

This is why their decisions seem fast.

They are not reacting to you, they are recognising patterns.

There is no single "investor mind."

There are only patterns.

THE FOUR SIGNALS INVESTORS SEE FIRST

Separate from the details, investors look for four early signals:

1. Coherence

Does story align with structure?

2. Capability

Does the team match the mission?

3. Efficiency

Is capital being used intelligently?

4. Trajectory

Is the company moving upward with stability?

Investors call this *momentum*.

But what they are actually reading is **structural coherence over time.**

THE SILENCE EXPLAINED

Silence is the most misunderstood investor signal.

Most founders interpret silence as rejection.

Often, it is not.

Silence usually means:

1. "The signal isn't clear."

Validation/capability/structure uncertain.

2. "The Gap is too wide or too distorted."

Not rejection, misalignment.

"Internal constraints, timing or fit."

And founders never hear these reasons.

Silence is rarely personal.

It is structural, logistical or sequencing-based.

WHAT INVESTORS RARELY SAY - BUT ALWAYS LOOK FOR

Investors almost never articulate the real filters:

- retention > revenue
- behaviour > narrative
- margin stability > top-line growth
- leadership maturity > charisma
- clarity > confidence
- capability > enthusiasm
- coherence > pitch polish
- Gap accuracy > ambition

Founders who understand these patterns stop pitching to impress and start communicating with structural clarity.

THE DIFFERENCE BETWEEN "NO" AND "NOT YET"

Understanding this difference changes founder psychology:

A **No** usually means:

- mandate mismatch
- sector not a fit
- risk profile incompatible
- investment thesis mismatched

A **Not Yet** means:

- validation needs strengthening
- model stability required
- structure not ready
- team capability gap
- narrative misaligned
- X-Factor not yet coherent

Most founders interpret **Not Yet** as **No**.

In reality, it is direction.

INSIDE THE INVESTMENT COMMITTEE (IC ROOM)

Inside an IC, the questions become sharper:

- "Where is the hidden risk?"
- "What Gap concerns us most?"

- "What is the cost to close it?"
- "Does leadership match the next 12–24 months?"
- "If we invest, are we amplifying coherence or amplifying instability?"

Notice what is absent:

no one asks about passion, effort or founder bravado.

They are assessing **structural readiness**, not emotional intensity.

MICRO EXAMPLES

Weak: "We're raising because we want to grow faster."

Strong: "We're raising to close the churn + onboarding Gap and strengthen retention before scaling."

Weak: "Investors didn't get it."

Strong: "Our story was ahead of our model mechanics, we need to realign narrative with reality."

MICRO EXERCISE

Investor Clarity Prompt

Answer these two questions in one sentence each:

"What is the Gap we are closing?"

"What will change structurally when we close it?"

If the answers are vague, the investor view will be unclear.

SEEING LIKE AN INVESTOR

You do not need to become an investor.

But you do need to understand how investors see:

- patterns
- risks
- Gaps
- capability
- timing
- ROI
- coherence

Once you see your venture through this lens, everything becomes clearer:

- your narrative sharpens
- your roadmap strengthens
- your capital strategy becomes grounded
- your team alignment improves
- your decisions accelerate
- your confidence stabilises

Investors do not expect perfection.

They expect coherence.

And coherence is entirely within your control.

CHAPTER 21

The Compass Inside the VC Mastermind

The Venture Compass is a powerful diagnostic and decision-making tool on its own. Many founders use it privately, within their team or as part of strategic planning. But for some founders, there comes a moment where clarity is not the challenge, it is structure, sequencing, capability and the need for a supportive environment where they can apply that clarity with consistency.

This is where the **VC Mastermind** sits.
Not as an additional layer on top of the Compass,
but as an ecosystem where the Compass becomes a **living practice**.

Inside the Mastermind, founders work with the Compass in real time:
- applying insights to their current stage
- refining their roadmap
- closing the highest-leverage Gaps
- strengthening leadership capability
- correcting psychological distortions
- stabilising structure
- sequencing capital and growth
- developing the capacity to move through complexity with confidence

The Mastermind exists for one reason:

some conversations require a room, not a report.

It brings founders into a structured environment where the Compass is used repeatedly, rhythmically and in community, turning clarity into capability, and capability into transformation.

AN EVERGREEN PATHWAY

The details of the Mastermind will evolve over time.

The rhythm, the curriculum and the tools will adapt as the broader ecosystem grows.

For that reason, this book only offers a light overview.

To explore the current version, visit:

www.theventurecompass.com

This link will always point to the latest information.

THE ROLE OF THE COMPASS INSIDE THE MASTERMIND

Inside the Mastermind, the Compass becomes:

- a shared map
- a common language
- a way to diagnose challenges
- a way to stabilise decision-making
- a way to correct founder-psychology distortion
- a way to sequence growth and capital
- a way to navigate the Gap with accuracy
- a way to build leadership maturity
- a structural foundation for capability development

The Compass shows founders where they are.

The Mastermind gives founders the **support, structure and accountability** needed to move through the Gap deliberately and consistently.

THE DEEPER SYSTEMS (LIGHT, CLEAN)

Book One introduces the map.

Book Two, the Systems Edition, reveals the deeper frameworks that sit beneath the Compass, including:

- the Capital–Growth–People execution tripod
- the Creation → Choices → Structure → Leverage → Legacy model
- deeper pattern-recognition tools
- advanced diagnostics
- leadership and narrative maturity frameworks
- structural and financial architectures that shape growth

These are explored at depth inside the Mastermind, where founders integrate them into their day-to-day leadership and long-term strategy.

This additional layer is not required for Book One —
but it becomes increasingly powerful as the venture grows.

WHY COMMUNITY MATTERS

Building a company is often isolating.

Founders carry weight long before they receive support.

They make decisions that affect others long before they have clarity.

They experience pressure long before they experience recognition.

A structured founder community breaks that isolation.

Inside the Mastermind, founders:

- surface blind spots safely
- learn through shared patterns
- correct misreads quickly
- validate decisions with other capable operators
- build leadership capacity
- gain perspective
- stay grounded and focused
- reduce psychological noise
- close Gaps faster and with better sequencing

Community is not comparison.
It is coherence, a shared environment where clarity compounds.

THE CHOICE BELONGS TO YOU

This book gives you the Compass, the map, the method and the structural logic to bring clarity to your venture. You may choose to apply it independently. Many founders do.

But if you ever want deeper structure, supported sequencing or a room of leaders who are walking the same path, the Mastermind is the natural next step, a place where the Compass becomes a **practice**, not just a framework.

For now, all you need to know is that support exists if you want it.

The map is yours.
The next steps are yours.
The journey is yours.

CHAPTER 22

Building a Stronger Venture
Using the Compass Method

The Venture Compass is more than a diagnostic. It is a way of building. A way of thinking. A way of leading. A way of making decisions that are grounded, coherent and proportionate to the stage of your venture.

By now, you have explored each quadrant, understood the X-Factor, seen how the Gap shapes momentum and learned how to turn clarity into movement. What remains is the deeper integration, using the Compass as a structural method for building a stronger, more resilient and more investable company.

The Compass becomes most powerful when it becomes a practice, not an event.

THE COMPASS AS A STRUCTURAL MINDSET
Most founders operate from instinct.
The Compass brings structure.
Most founders move from urgency.
The Compass brings sequence.
Most founders interpret challenges emotionally.
The Compass brings pattern-recognition.
Most founders respond to symptoms.

The Compass reveals the system beneath them.

When founders shift from reactive problem-solving to Compass-driven structural thinking, decision quality improves, psychological noise decreases and capability expands.

This is where the Compass becomes a **method**, not just a map.

THE THREE PRINCIPLES OF THE COMPASS METHOD

Three principles anchor this way of building:

1. See the system, not the symptom

Every visible problem is a surface expression of deeper forces.

Examples:

- churn may be a structure or onboarding issue
- slow growth may be a validation issue
- hiring problems may be a role clarity issue
- investor friction may be a narrative or X-Factor issue

The Compass teaches founders to ask:

"What system is this challenge coming from?"

This question dissolves confusion and accelerates accuracy.

2. Sequence beats intensity

More effort does not create more progress.

Better sequencing does.

Examples:

Weak: "Let's grow faster."

Strong: "Let's close the retention Gap before adding top-of-funnel volume."

Weak: "We need capital."

Strong: "We need capital *after* we stabilise unit economics."

Effort creates movement.

Sequence creates momentum.

3. Alignment compounds

When validation, timing, structure, culture, people, capital and narrative move together, performance multiplies.

Alignment increases:

- execution quality
- speed
- trust
- investor readiness
- team stability
- resilience

This is the compounding effect of coherence.

Alignment is not a belief, it is a design choice.

HOW THE COMPASS EVOLVES WITH YOUR COMPANY

As your business evolves, so does the Compass.

Early stage

- validation
- messaging
- pricing
- early structure

Traction stage

- growth mechanics
- retention
- unit economics
- team alignment

Scale stage

- leadership maturity
- structure
- capital sequencing
- operational depth

Later stage

- integration
- governance
- responsibility
- advanced capital architecture

The Compass adapts as the venture adapts.

THE COMPASS INSIDE YOUR LEADERSHIP

When founders internalise Compass logic, several shifts occur:

- fewer reactive decisions
- more grounded communication
- disciplined prioritisation
- clearer team alignment
- better investor conversations
- calmer leadership presence
- deeper understanding of capability and capacity
- sequencing as a default, not an exception

Leadership becomes less about carrying weight and more about **designing movement.**

STRUCTURAL RHYTHMS THAT STRENGTHEN THE METHOD

To embed the Compass into your operating rhythm, adopt these simple practices:

Quarterly Compass Review
Reassess the quadrants every 12 weeks.
Mark the movement.
Identify the new Gap.

Monthly Pattern Scan
Observe where effort feels heavy, where decisions stall, where friction is rising.

Weekly Alignment Rhythm
Short check-ins to ensure clarity on priorities, decisions and commitments.

Narrative Calibration

Revisit narrative whenever strategy shifts.

Coherence is leadership.

Founder Calibration

Ask regularly:

"Where is my energy out of alignment with the stage of the business?"

Your internal alignment shapes the company's external performance.

MICRO EXAMPLES

Weak: "We're struggling with execution."

Strong: "Our structure gap around ownership is slowing decisions, we're addressing that first."

Weak: "We need more leads."

Strong: "We need stronger activation and retention before increasing acquisition."

MICRO EXERCISE

Alignment Prompt

Write one sentence:

"The structural move that will create the most momentum in the next 90 days is…"

If you can't complete it clearly, revisit the Compass.

THE BUSINESS FEELS DIFFERENT WHEN BUILT THIS WAY

Founders often notice a shift when the Compass becomes a practice:

- clarity increases
- noise decreases
- execution steadies
- culture strengthens
- team alignment improves
- decisions become easier
- investor confidence grows
- the X-Factor becomes visible

This shift is not abstract.

It is architectural, the business begins to move as one coherent system.

THE COMPASS IS A WAY OF BUILDING

A venture built with Compass logic is:

- well-designed
- grounded
- coherent
- resilient
- capable of sustainable growth
- aligned with its long-term potential

You do not need perfection to build a great company.

You need structure, clarity and sequence.

The Compass gives you all three.

THE FOUNDER'S PATH FORWARD

Building a venture requires courage, perspective and the capacity to navigate uncertainty without losing momentum.

The Compass does not remove the uncertainty.
It simply gives you a way to navigate through it.

Return to it whenever things feel noisy, heavy or unclear.
It will show you where to look.
It will show you what matters.
It will show you the path from current reality to potential reality.

The journey is yours.
The Compass simply gives you a map.

CHAPTER 23

Closing Thoughts: You Have a Map Now

Every founder begins with possibility. Along the way, complexity arrives. Pressure arrives. Uncertainty arrives. The work becomes heavier than expected and the path more tangled than imagined. What disappears first in this process is often the thing founders need most: clarity.

The Venture Compass was created to restore that clarity, to give founders a structure for seeing what is real, what is possible and what it will take to bridge the distance between the two. It offers a way to remove guesswork, reduce psychological distortion and make decisions with calm, grounded precision.

By now, you have seen that the Compass is not only a diagnostic. It is a navigation system, a way to understand the structural forces shaping your venture, the patterns influencing performance and the sequence required to close the Gaps that matter most.

You now understand:

- the nine forces that determine trajectory
- the X-Factor that binds them
- the psychological distortions that blur perception
- the structural patterns investors read

- the ROI logic behind Gap closure
- the principles that turn clarity into movement
- the rhythm that turns movement into momentum

You have a map.

A way to see your current reality honestly.

A way to imagine your potential reality clearly.

A way to understand the Gap objectively, without underestimating or overstretching it.

Closing the Gap is not an emotional journey.

It is a structural one, a sequence of intentional moves, well-timed decisions and capability-building moments that shift the venture from where it is to where it could be.

A founder with clarity can act with confidence.

A founder with structure can act with coherence.

A founder with both can change the trajectory of their venture permanently.

Use this Compass whenever the business feels noisy, unclear, or heavy.

Use it whenever you reach a new stage, a new challenge or a new opportunity.

Use it to align your team, refine your strategy, recalibrate your narrative and design your next move.

You are not expected to know everything.

You are expected to move with intention.

You have a map now, a way to navigate uncertainty with confidence and coherence.

Use it well. The distance between where you are and where you could be is your opportunity.

FURTHER EXPLORATION — TOOLS FOR FOUNDERS WHO WANT TO GO DEEPER

The Compass is the simplest expression of a deeper ecosystem of tools, models and structural frameworks. For founders who want to explore further, the following areas often complement the Compass:

- **Marlee (formerly Fingerprint for Success)** - cognitive patterns, blind spots, team dynamics
- **Creative Paradigm** - current reality, vision, bridge and Gap
- **Capital–Growth–People Tripod** - the execution foundation beneath the Compass
- **Creation–Choices–Structure–Leverage–Legacy Model** - the deeper architecture underpinning founder evolution
- **Jobs-to-Be-Done** - behavioural analysis of customer decision-making
- **Helmer's Seven Powers** - structural competitive advantage
- **Category Mapping** - understanding category dynamics and positioning
- **Leadership Maturity Models** - deepening founder capability and relational intelligence
- **Multi-Capital Integration Tools** - responsibility, coherence and system alignment
- **Cross-Quadrant Diagnostic Templates** - revealing patterns, interactions and structural coherence

These tools are explored in far greater depth in Book Two, the Systems Edition, and form part of the advanced toolkit used inside the VC Mastermind.

AFTERWORD

This book is the entry point into the Venture Compass™. It gives founders the map, the method and a practical way to understand the structural forces shaping their business. The deeper systems that sit beneath the Compass, the frameworks, diagnostic tools, pattern libraries and advanced methodologies, belong in the companion volume and in the lived practice of working closely with founders inside the Mastermind.

If you choose to explore that path, the Systems Edition offers a richer and more detailed body of work that reveals the deeper architecture beneath the Compass.

ABOUT THE AUTHORS

Mark Falzon is an entrepreneur, investor and author with more than forty-five years of experience building, scaling and advising ventures across Australia, Asia and the United States. His work spans regenerative capital design, food security, health innovation, clean energy, leadership development and venture strategy. As co-founder of MAD and co-creator of the Venture Compass™ framework, Mark brings a unique blend of systems thinking, operational depth and practical wisdom to founders navigating complex, high-growth environments. He is known for helping leaders find clarity in uncertainty and building ventures that are coherent, purposeful and structurally sound.

Mac Christopherson is a strategist, investor and venture architect with a career spanning multiple industries and growth stages. As co-founder of MAD and co-creator of the Venture Compass™, Mac specialises in capital architecture, financial strategy and organisational design. He is known for turning complexity into clear structural logic and for designing the systems that allow founders, teams and capital to move coherently together. Mac's work combines analytical depth with a commitment to founder development, enabling leaders to scale with clarity while he focuses on the long-term design of the venture itself.

Together, **Mark and Mac** bring decades of lived experience across hundreds of ventures. Their work has shaped founders, teams and ecosystems around the world, and the Venture Compass™ represents the distillation of their shared insights into a simple, powerful and practical navigation system for founders everywhere.